FLAVORS FROM THE FRENCH
MEDITERRANEAN

Editorial Director: Kate Mascaro
Editor: Helen Adedotun
Translated from the French by Julia Chalkley
Design: OFF/Olivier Fontvieille and Anne Ponscarme
Copyediting: Wendy Sweetser
Typesetting: Gravemaker+Scott
Proofreading: Nicole Foster
Color Separation: IGS, L'Isle d'Espagnac, France
Printed in China by Toppan Leefung

Originally published in French
as *Ma Méditerranée # Cuisine*
© Flammarion, S.A., Paris, 2015

English-language edition
© Flammarion, S.A., Paris, 2016

87, quai Panhard et Levassor
75647 Paris Cedex 13

editions.flammarion.com

16 17 18 3 2 1

ISBN: 978-2-08-020251-2

Legal Deposit: 03/2016

Gérald Passedat

FLAVORS FROM THE FRENCH
MEDITERRANEAN

Photography by Richard Haughton

Flammarion

GÉRALD PASSEDAT: THE SHOP

The ingredients used in this book that are marked with an asterisk (*) are available from The Shop, Gérald Passedat's online delicatessen.

His product range includes spice mixes such as Curry Fakir or Pain d'Épicier, his own brand of extra virgin olive oil, as well as flavored vinegars, including mango and lemon.

The complete range can be viewed and ordered on www.passadat.fr/boutique. International shipping is available.

CONTENTS

MAIN COURSES

DESSERTS

INTRODUCTION

I was born in Marseille, overlooking the Mediterranean Sea.

Its landscapes and sunlight have made me who I am today.

I have fond childhood memories of the women and men in my family: my grandmothers Lucie and Mélanie, my aunts Nia and Guite, my grandfather Barthélemy, and my uncle Jésus—all passionate cooks who helped me develop my sense of taste and who taught me how to express myself. **When I was twelve years old I had a life-changing experience at dinner one evening at the restaurant of renowned chef Alain Chapel**: I knew then that I would become a chef and that one day I would gain three Michelin stars.

My cuisine is firmly rooted in the south of France. In the south, like Marseille, that means an intermingling of the culture of a port with the salty spray of the sea as it drifts in from afar, bringing with it all the fantasies one imagines from constantly scanning distant horizons.

In this book, I share my own family recipes and my signature cuisine, bursting with color and flavor, in which olive oil and garlic remain the essential ingredients and which gives pride of place to fresh vegetables and fish.

This book is also an invitation to discover and experiment with my favorite ingredients: from brousse du Rove, the delicate, ultra-fresh goats' curds from an ancient breed of goat raised in Le Rove, to bottarga, dubbed "Mediterranean caviar," with its unique salty flavor. You can also make tapenade (olive paste), anchoïade (anchovy sauce), soupe au pistou (vegetable soup with pesto), aïgo (garlic and bread soup), and bouille abaisse (fish stew), to name but a few of the culinary delights from the south featured in this book.

I hope that you will truly enjoy this voyage to the French Mediterranean.

APPETIZERS

SEA BASS
AIOLI

AÏOLI DE LOUP

Ingredients

4 sea bass fillets,
 weighing 4 oz. (120 g)
 each, skin removed
1 medium potato
3 cloves garlic
Scant ½ cup (100 ml)
 milk
1 egg yolk
¼ cup (50 ml) Passedat
 olive oil*
2 orange carrots
2 yellow carrots
1 large white turnip
½ medium celeriac
2 sticks celery
2 small leeks
1 bouquet garni
2 eggs
Salt, pepper

Serves 4 | *Preparation time: 45 minutes* | *Cooking time: 12 minutes*

Peel and roughly **chop** the potato, **boil** in salted water until tender. **Drain** thoroughly, then **sieve** or **mash** with a fork. **Allow to cool** completely.

Peel the garlic cloves and **boil** in the milk for 2 minutes, **drain** and **crush** with a fork. **Mix** the mashed potato in a bowl with the garlic and egg yolk. **Season** with salt and pepper to taste, then gradually **whisk** in the olive oil until the mixture is the consistency of mayonnaise. **Reserve** in the refrigerator to garnish the dish.

Peel the carrots, turnip, and celeriac, **pull** any "strings" off the celery sticks, and **trim** the leeks. **Slice** the vegetables lengthways and **cook** them in boiling water until cooked through; **drain** and **reserve**.

Poach the sea bass fillets with the bouquet garni for 10 minutes in a court bouillon or water to cover, then **drain**. **Cook** the eggs in boiling water for 7 minutes, **refresh**, **peel**, and **cut** in half.

Arrange the vegetables on individual plates, **add** a fillet of fish and half an egg. **Garnish** with quenelle-shaped spoonfuls of the aioli.

CHEF'S NOTE
The mashed potato needs to be completely cold for the aioli to emulsify without separating.

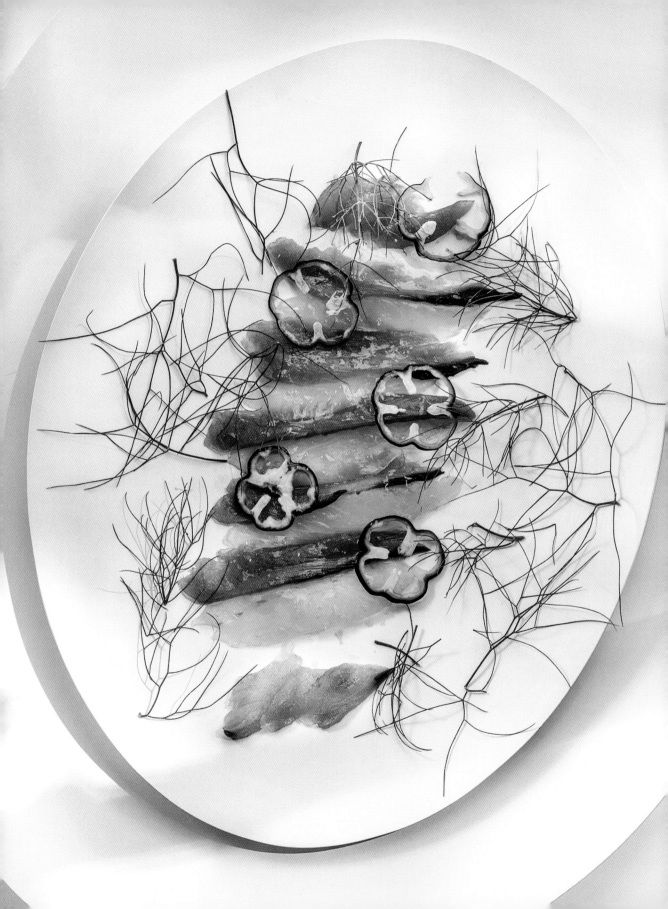

LEERFISH, BONITO, AND SEA BREAM CARPACCIO

CARPACCIO DE LICHE, PÉLAMIDE ET DORADE

Ingredients

1 leerfish (or tuna) fillet, weighing 7 oz. (200 g)

1 sea bream fillet, weighing 7 oz. (200 g)

1 Atlantic bonito fillet, weighing 7 oz. (200 g)

2 purple bell peppers

1 sprig fresh wild fennel (or Florence fennel tops)

2 lemons

¼ cup (50 ml) Passedat olive oil*

Fleur de sel, pepper

Serves 4 | *Preparation time: 30 minutes*

Skin and slice the fillets of fish thinly and arrange them neatly on a serving dish. Wash the bell peppers, cut them into very thin slices, deseed, and place the slices on and around the fish.

Wash the sprig of fennel, remove the fronds from the stalk, and lay them over the fish.

Zest the lemons over the fish, drizzle with the olive oil, and season with salt and pepper.

CHEF'S NOTE

Serve at room temperature so that the flavor of the fish can be enjoyed at its best.

ASPARAGUS WITH ANCHOÏADE

ASPERGES EN ANCHOÏADE

Ingredients

24 green asparagus
  stalks
1 lemon
5 tablespoons
  Passedat olive oil*
1 small bunch cilantro
1 scallion
3 ½ oz. (100 g) anchovy
  fillets in oil
¾ oz. (20 g) black olives
½ cup (1 oz./30 g) bread
  crumbs
Scant ½ cup (100 ml)
  milk
1 clove garlic
Salt, pepper

Serves 4 | *Preparation time: 1 hour* | *Cooking time: 30 minutes*

Peel the asparagus stalks and **divide** them into 2 bundles. **Tie up** each one with string. **Trim** the stalks to the same length so the bundles will remain upright in a saucepan. **Peel** the lemon, keeping the peel.

Heat 4 tablespoons of the olive oil in a tall saucepan and **stand** the asparagus in it. **Add** the cilantro, lemon peel, and scallion, and enough water to cover the base of the pan. **Let cook** for 25 minutes. If the water evaporates, **add** more, checking the pan at regular intervals.

Rinse the anchovies and olives. **Soak** the bread crumbs in the milk, then **squeeze out** the excess moisture. **Peel** the garlic.

Put the anchovies, olives, garlic, and bread crumbs in a food processor, **add** a splash of olive oil, and **process** until smooth. **Add** salt and pepper to taste. **Set aside** in a cool place.

Arrange the asparagus on a serving dish and **serve** with a quenelle-shaped spoonful of the anchovy mixture (*anchoïade*).

PURPLE ARTICHOKE BARIGOULE

ARTICHAUTS VIOLETS EN BARIGOULE

Ingredients

20 small, purple
  artichokes
1 lemon
2 shallots
2 cloves garlic
2 pearl onions
½ cup (3 ½ oz./
  100 g) smoked
  bacon, cut into cubes
  (*lardons*)
Scant ¼ cup (50 ml)
  dry white wine
1 orange
¼ teaspoon fennel
  seeds
2 star anise
1 sprig parsley
4 ¼ cups (1 liter)
  vegetable stock
1 small bunch chervil
Salt, pepper

Serves 4 | *Preparation time: 1 hour* | *Cooking time: 25 minutes*

Juice the lemon and **add** the juice to a bowl of cold water. To prepare the artichokes, **remove** any tough outer leaves, then **cut off** the top third of the artichoke to reveal the inner purple leaves. **Remove** these with a spoon, then **pull out** the hairy choke and discard. **Immerse** the artichokes in the bowl of acidulated water to prevent them discoloring.

Peel and **chop** the shallots, **peel** and **crush** the garlic, and **peel** and **slice** the pearl onions in rounds. **Put** them all in a deep saucepan with the smoked bacon cubes.

Sweat over a medium heat until the vegetables have softened. **Moisten** with the wine and **bubble** until the wine has reduced.

Drain the artichokes and **add** them to the saucepan. **Remove** the zest from the orange in thin strips with a potato peeler and **add** it to the pan with the fennel seeds, star anise, and parsley. **Add** the stock and **season** with salt and pepper. **Allow to simmer** for 20 minutes.

Roughly **chop** the chervil and **sprinkle** it over just before serving.

EGGPLANT WITH GARRIGUES-STYLE GOAT CHEESE

AUBERGINES ET CHÈVRE DES GARRIGUES

Ingredients

4 eggplants
Passedat olive oil*
1 ¾ cups (14 oz./400 g)
  tomato sauce and
  1 ¼ cups (7 oz./200 g)
  tomato concassé
  (see Tomatoes Three
  Ways, p. 56)
7 oz. (200 g) fresh
  goat cheese, sliced
1 bunch basil
5 ¼ oz. (150 g)
  Parmesan shavings
Salt, pepper

Serves 4 | Preparation time: 50 minutes | Cooking time: 30 minutes

Preheat the oven to 300°F (150°C/Gas mark 2).

Wash the eggplants and **slice** them lengthways on a mandolin, into strips ¼ in. (5 mm) thick.

Brush them with olive oil, then **season** with salt and pepper. **Preheat** a ribbed grill pan and **color** them on both sides. **Blot** the slices with paper towel to remove any excess oil, **transfer** to a baking sheet, and **cook** in the oven for 20 minutes.

Put two slices of eggplant in a casserole. **Coat** them with some of the tomato sauce, then some of the chopped tomatoes. **Place** two slices of goat cheese and several basil leaves on top, then **repeat** the layers until the casserole is three quarters full.

Finish with the Parmesan shavings and **place** the casserole in the oven until the top is well browned.

PROVENÇAL TOMATO SANDWICH

BAGNAT DE TOMATES

Ingredients

1 focaccia measuring
10 × 10 in.
(25 × 25 cm)
2 green zebra tomatoes
2 pineapple tomatoes
1 small, green Marseille
bell pepper
1 red onion
1 little gem lettuce
1 bunch basil
3 oz. (80 g) green beans
Scant 1 cup (200 ml)
tomato vinaigrette
(see p. 57)
¾ cup (150 g) tuna in oil
¾ oz. (20 g) black olives
6 anchovy fillets
2 teaspoons (10 g)
capers or caper buds
2 hard-boiled eggs
Passedat olive oil*
Salt, pepper

Serves 4 | *Preparation time: 20 minutes* | *Cooking time: 10 minutes*

Cut the focaccia in half horizontally.

Slice the tomatoes, bell pepper, and red onion. **Remove** the stalks from the little gem lettuce and the basil. **Blanch** the green beans in boiling water for 10 minutes, then **refresh** under cold running water.

Moisten both of the cut sides of the focaccia well with tomato vinaigrette; **spread** the lettuce leaves over the bottom half.

Arrange the tomatoes, onion, and bell pepper on top of the lettuce, then **add** the green beans, flaked tuna, olives, and anchovies. **Sprinkle** with the capers and **add** the basil leaves. **Push** the hard-boiled eggs through a sieve and then **sprinkle** over, **season** with salt and pepper, and finally **drizzle** with olive oil.

Place the other half of the focaccia on top and **cut** into four equal portions.

CARPACCIO OF OCTOPUS FROM THE CALANQUE DU CONTREBANDIER

CARPACCIO DE POULPE,
CALANQUE DU CONTREBANDIER

Ingredients

1 cleaned octopus,
    weighing
    approximately
    2 lb. 3 oz. (1 kg)
1 shallot
3 ½ oz. (100 g) carrot
¼ leek
½ stick celery
4 teaspoons Passedat
    mango vinegar*
Passedat olive oil*
1 lemon
1 lime
4 red radishes
1 small bunch dill
Salt, pepper

Serves 4 | *Preparation time: 1 hour 30 minutes* | *Cooking time: 1 hour 15 minutes*

Roll up the octopus into a cylindrical shape. **Tie** firmly with string. **Place** it in a saucepan and **cover** with cold water. **Add** the shallot, carrot, leek, and celery and **bring to a boil. Lower** the heat and **cover**, **simmer** for 1 hour 15 minutes.

When cooked, **drain** the octopus, **allow to cool** a little, then **remove** the string and **slice** the octopus into thin rounds.

Arrange the slices on a serving dish and **dress** with the mango vinegar, a splash of olive oil, and salt and pepper to taste. **Zest** the lemon and lime over the surface and **add** a squeeze or two of lemon juice.

Cut the radishes into quarters and **arrange** them on top. Finally, **decorate** with fronds of dill.

CHEF'S NOTE
This dish should be eaten as soon as it is cooked.

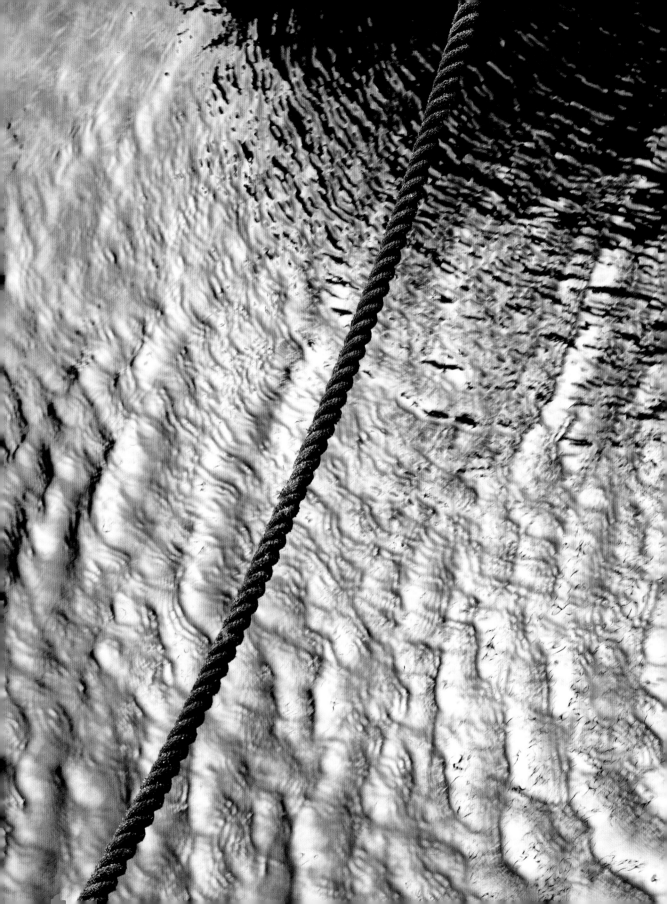

GRILLED SARDINES WITH EGGPLANT

SARDINES GRILLÉES AUX AUBERGINES

Ingredients

12 sardines

2 eggplants

Scant ½ cup (100 ml)
   Passedat olive oil*

1 small bunch thyme,
   with flowers if
   possible

1 lemon

Salt, pepper

Serves 4 | *Preparation time: 1 hour 45 minutes* | *Cooking time: about 1 hour 30 minutes*

Preheat the oven to 300°F (150°C/Gas mark 2).

Wash the eggplants, **remove** their stalks, and **brush** them with olive oil. **Season** with salt and pepper, then **wrap** them in aluminum foil and **cook** in the oven for 1 hour 30 minutes.

Clean and **remove** the heads from the sardines. **Cut** diagonal slices down each side with a sharp knife.

Place the sardines on a plate and **season** with salt, pepper, and a splash of olive oil. **Tuck** tiny sprigs of the thyme into the slashes.

When the eggplants are cooked, **cut** them lengthways into thin slices. **Place** three slices on each plate, **brush** with olive oil, then **season** with salt, pepper, and some thyme leaves.

Preheat a grill pan and **cook** the sardines for 30 seconds on each side. **Arrange** them on the eggplant slices and **zest** the lemon over them, then **add** a squeeze of lemon juice. **Garnish** with the thyme flowers.

G R I L L E D
RAZOR CLAMS
W I T H
BOTTARGA

POUTARGUE ET COUTEAUX GRILLÉS

Ingredients

4 razor clams

2 lemons

16 large white button
mushrooms

1 lime

2 teaspoons (10 g)
flying fish roe

2 teaspoons (10 g)
mullet roe

1 small bunch parsley

1 small bunch basil

Passedat olive oil*

½ bottarga (dried
mullet roe)

Salt, pepper

Serves 4 | *Preparation time: 20 minutes* | *Soaking time:*
30 minutes | *Cooking time: about 5 minutes*

Soak the razor clams in cold water to cover for 30 minutes to extract
any sand.

Zest the lemons, reserving the zest, and **squeeze** the juice.

Peel the mushrooms, **toss** them in half of the lemon juice, then
slice them finely on a mandolin. **Arrange** them on four individual
plates.

Preheat a ribbed grill pan. **Place** the razor clams on the pan and
cook briefly on each side until they open.

Peel the lime, removing all pith and membrane, and **cut** the
flesh into small dice.

Arrange the fish roes, herbs, lemon zest, and diced lime evenly
over the mushrooms, **season** with salt and pepper, then **add** a drizzle
of olive oil and a splash of the remaining lemon juice. **Place** a razor
clam on the edge of each plate and lastly finely **shave** the bottarga
into thin slices over the plates.

C H E F ' S   N O T E
The bottarga should look plump; it is traditionally encased in bees' wax.

SHELLFISH STUFFED WITH HERBS AND GINGER

COQUILLAGES FARCIS

Ingredients

4 hard-shell clams

20 carpet-shell clams

20 cockles

16 small lagoon cockles

3 ¼ oz. (90 g) sliced country bread

½ cup (1 oz./30 g) chopped thyme

¼ cup (½ oz./15 g) chopped rosemary

Scant ½ cup (⅔ oz./20 g) chopped basil

Scant ½ cup (⅔ oz./20 g) chopped cilantro

2 tablespoons cognac

1 tablespoon (½ oz./15 g) lemon zest

1 tablespoon lemon juice

Generous ½ cup (140 ml) Passedat olive oil*

1 oz. (30 g) peeled, finely chopped garlic

½ oz. (15 g) peeled, finely chopped root ginger

10 oz. (300 g) seaweed, for decoration

Salt, pepper

Serves 4 | *Preparation time: 25 minutes* | *Soaking time: 30 minutes* | *Cooking time: a few minutes*

Soak all the shellfish in a bowl of cold water for 30 minutes to extract any sand.

Toast the country bread and **remove** the crusts. **Chop** finely and **place** in a mixing bowl. **Add** all the chopped herbs.

Warm the cognac in a ladle or small pan, **remove** from the heat and **set** it **alight**. Once the flames have subsided, **add** the cognac to the herb and bread stuffing mixture.

Add the lemon zest and juice, then the olive oil, garlic, and ginger. **Season** with salt and pepper to taste and **mix** everything together.

Cook the shellfish in a splash of olive oil in a covered pan over a high heat for a few seconds, until they have all opened up. **Allow to cool** a little, then **remove** the shellfish meat, reserving one half of the shells.

Preheat the oven to 350°F (180°C/Gas mark 4).

Return the shellfish meat to the half shells and **put** a spoonful of stuffing on top. **Spread** them **out** in a single layer on a baking sheet and **put** in the oven for a few minutes to heat through.

Serve the shellfish on a bed of seaweed.

CHEF'S NOTE
A small salad can be served on the side consisting of finely chopped seaweed dressed with a shallot reduction, white wine vinegar, lemon juice, and olive oil, garnished with pine nuts and fresh dill.

MOZZARELLA-STUFFED ZUCCHINI FLOWERS

FLEURS DE COURGETTE FARCIES
À LA MOZZARELLA

Ingredients
20 zucchini flowers

For the tomato sauce
8 plum tomatoes
2 shallots
1 clove garlic
Scant ¼ cup (50 ml)
   Passedat olive oil*
1 teaspoon tomato
   paste
3 sprigs thyme

For the stuffing
   and decoration
10 oz. (300 g)
   mozzarella
1 small bunch basil
1 lemon
A few hyssop flowers
Salt, pepper

Serves 4 | *Preparation time: 45 minutes* | *Cooking time: 30 minutes*

To make the tomato sauce, **wash** the tomatoes, **remove** their stalks, and **cut** a cross in the base of each one with a small knife to make them easier to peel. **Immerse** the tomatoes in boiling water for a few seconds, **drain**, and immediately **place** in cold water. **Drain** again and **slip off** the skins. **Quarter** the tomatoes, **remove** the cores and **scoop out** the pulp. **Reserve** both the pulp and the tomato flesh in separate bowls.

 Chop the shallots, **crush** the garlic, and **sweat** them in a pan with a splash of the olive oil. **Add** the reserved tomato pulp, tomato paste, and the thyme. **Cover** the pan and **cook** for 20 minutes, then **pass through** a vegetable mill. **Set** aside.

To make the stuffing and decoration, **cut** a few small wedges from the reserved tomato flesh and mozzarella. **Reserve** these for decorating the finished dish. **Dice** the rest of the tomato flesh and mozzarella and **chop** the basil leaves.

Mix the diced tomato and mozzarella in a bowl with the basil. **Zest** the lemon into the bowl, and **season** the mixture with the rest of the olive oil, adding salt and pepper to taste.

Preheat the oven to 300°F (150°C/Gas mark 2). **Open up** the zucchini flowers and **remove** the stamens, then **fill** them with the stuffing mixture, using a spoon. **Arrange** them in a gratin dish, **pour** over the tomato sauce, and **cook** for 10 minutes.

Garnish with the reserved tomato and mozzarella wedges and the hyssop flowers before serving.

O C T O P U S
A N D
J O L S
T E M P U R A

P O U L P E   E T   J O L S   E N   T E M P U R A

Ingredients

1 octopus, ready
   cooked, weighing
   approximately
   1 lb. 2 oz. (500 g)
7 oz. (200 g) jols (see
   Chef's Note below),
   or use sprats or
   baby smelt
1 ½ cups (5 ¼ oz./150 g)
   tempura flour
   (or all-purpose flour)
¾ cup (180 ml) water
1 small bunch parsley
1 small bunch dill
1 lemon
4 ¼ cups (1 liter)
   grapeseed oil
Salt, pepper

Serves 4 | *Preparation time: 30 minutes | Cooking time: 5 minutes*

To make the tempura batter, **whisk** the flour and water together in a mixing bowl until smooth. **Reserve.**

Cut the octopus tentacles into large slices. **Wash** the jols under cold running water, then **place** on paper towel to drain. **Wash** the parsley and dill and **remove** the stalks. **Juice** the lemon.

Heat the oil in a heavy, deep pan or deep-fat fryer to 350°F (180°C).

One at a time, **dip** the pieces of octopus into the tempura batter to coat them, using a pair of large tongs, and then **lower** them into the hot oil. **Fry** for approximately 3 minutes and then **drain** on a plate lined with paper towel. **Repeat** with the jols, but only fry them for 1 ½ minutes.

Sprinkle the fried fish with the lemon juice. **Season** with salt and pepper and **scatter** over the chopped herbs.

C H E F ' S   N O T E
Jols are small fish from the Marseille area that are eaten whole.

SKATE-FILLED
ZUCCHINI

COURGETTES FARCIES À L'AILE DE RAIE

Ingredients

6 zucchini

10 oz. (300 g) skate
  wings

4 ¼ cups (1 liter) sheep
  milk

1 large potato, peeled
  and roughly chopped

1 lemon preserved
  in salt

4 teaspoons (20 g)
  caper buds

1 small bunch parsley

1 small bunch chives

⅔ cup (140 g) sheep
  yogurt

1 lemon

Passedat olive oil*

Salt, pepper

Serves 4 | *Preparation time: 30 minutes* | *Cooking time: 15 minutes*

Wash the zucchini, **cut** them in half lengthways, and **scoop out** the seeds with a melon baller. **Blanch** the zucchini in salted water for 4 minutes, then **refresh** under cold running water. **Reserve**.

Poach the skate wings in the sheep milk for 10 minutes over a medium heat. **Cook** the potato in boiling, salted water, then **drain**.

Soak the preserved lemon in water for a few minutes to remove the salt, **drain**, then **cut** in half and **scoop out** the pith and flesh. **Cut** the rind into thin julienne strips.

Cut a few caper buds in half and **reserve** with some of the parsley leaves to garnish the finished dish. **Chop** the remaining capers and parsley with the chives.

Remove the skin and bones from the skate wings and **flake** the flesh into a bowl. **Crush** the potato and **add** to the bowl with the yogurt, chopped herbs, capers, and preserved lemon. **Zest** the fresh lemon into the bowl and then **squeeze** the juice and **add** this as well. **Mix** everything together, adding salt and pepper to taste.

Stuff the zucchini with the mixture, using a spoon, then **garnish** with the halved caper buds and parsley leaves, and **drizzle** with olive oil. **Serve** cold.

S P I C Y **S E A B A S S**
C E V I C H E

MARINADE COMME UN CÉVICHE

Ingredients

10 oz. (300 g) sea bass
fillets, skin removed

For the hot chili sauce

2 tablespoons (30 ml)
lime juice

2 tablespoons (30 ml)
water

2 tablespoons (30 ml)
fish stock

Generous ½ cup
(1 oz./30 g) chopped
cilantro

Generous 1 teaspoon
(6 g) salt

½ teaspoon (3 g)
Espelette chili powder

2 teaspoons (10 g)
chopped root ginger

2 teaspoons (10 g)
chopped garlic

For the pickled
vegetables

Generous ⅔ cup (140 g)
full fat yogurt

1 pinch Espelette chili
powder

1 beet

1 bulb fennel

1 stick celery

1 in. (2.5 cm) piece
root ginger

¼ red onion

2 tablespoons
Passedat olive oil*

Scant 1 cup (200 ml)
white Pineau des
Charentes vinegar

For the ceviche

20 cockles

Scant ¼ cup (50 ml)
dry white wine

2 bay leaves

1 sprig thyme

4 crab claws, cooked

2 teaspoons (10 g)
fleur de sel

Salt, pepper

Serves 4 | *Preparation time: 45 minutes* | *Marinating time:
5 minutes* | *Cooking time: 5 minutes*

To make the hot chili sauce, **mix** all the ingredients together. **Reserve**
in a cool place.

Prepare the pickled vegetables. **Strain** the yogurt through
muslin to drain off the whey (about 15 minutes). **Mix** the strained
yogurt with the chili powder and **add** salt and pepper to taste.

Wash the beet, fennel, celery, ginger, and red onion. **Peel** the
beet, ginger, and red onion and **remove** any "strings" from the celery.
Slice the vegetables thinly and **shape** into rounds, rectangles, or
lozenges, as you prefer. **Grate** or finely **chop** the ginger.

Put the vegetables and ginger in a pan with the olive oil and
vinegar. **Cover** the pan and **cook** for 1 ½ minutes. **Drain** and **reserve**.

To prepare the ceviche, **cut** the fillets of sea bass into cubes
and **marinate** in the hot chili sauce for 5 minutes to "cook" it as for a
ceviche, before assembling the finished dish.

Cook the cockles for a few minutes in a skillet with the white
wine, bay leaves, and thyme until all the shells have opened. **Crack**
the crab claws.

Arrange cubes of sea bass, a crab claw, and a selection of the
pickled vegetables on each plate.

Form quenelle shapes of spiced yogurt with two spoons and
garnish each plate with them. **Sprinkle** *fleur de sel* and **drizzle** a little
olive oil over each serving, and finally **add** the cockles.

EGGPLANT TERRINE

POUPETON D'AUBERGINE

Ingredients

2 lb. 3 oz. (1 kg)
    eggplants
Passedat olive oil*
8 eggs
6 tablespoons (90 ml)
    whipping cream
2 tablespoons ground
    cumin
Salt, pepper

Serves 4 | *Preparation time: 30 minutes* | *Cooking time: 3 hours*

Preheat the oven to 325°F (160°C/Gas mark 3).

Wash the eggplants and **remove** the stalks. **Rub** them with olive oil and **season** with salt and pepper. **Wrap** them in aluminum foil and **bake** for 1 hour 30 minutes.

When cooked, **cut** the eggplants in half and **squeeze** them gently to remove excess moisture. **Remove** the skin. **Place** in a food processor, **add** the eggs, cream, and cumin, and **reduce** to a purée. **Check** the seasoning.

Increase the oven temperature to 350°F (180°C/Gas mark 4). **Line** a terrine dish with parchment paper and **pour** the mixture in. Tightly **cover** the dish with aluminum foil and **stand** it in a bain-marie. **Cook** in the oven for 1 hour 30 minutes.

CHEF'S NOTE
This terrine tastes best when served at room temperature.

MACKEREL
SERVED IN
A SAVORY
LEMON BROTH

MAQUEREAU EN NAGE DE CITRON

Ingredients
3 mackerel

For the broth
½ carrot
¾ oz. (20 g) celery
1 ½ oz. (40 g) leek
Passedat olive oil*
1 lemon
4 ½ tablespoons (65 ml)
    Passedat lemon
    vinegar*
Scant ¼ cup (50 ml)
    white wine
1 sprig parsley
2 black peppercorns
2 ½ cups (600 ml) water

To complete the dish
1 yellow carrot
1 orange carrot
1 white carrot
Chive flowers
½ black radish
A few tiny florets
    purple cauliflower
A few chives
A few sprigs dill
A few sprigs chervil

Serves 4 | *Preparation time: 45 minutes* | *Cooking time: 30 minutes*

To make the broth, roughly **chop** the carrot, celery, and leek. **Put** them in a large saucepan with a splash of olive oil and **sweat** over a low heat. **Peel** the lemon thinly and **add** the peel to the pan with the lemon vinegar, wine, parsley, peppercorns, and water. **Increase** the heat and **boil** steadily for 30 minutes, then **strain** through a fine-mesh sieve and **reserve** the broth.

Clean the mackerel, **remove** the heads, and **wash** them. **Fillet** the fish, pulling out any remaining bones with tweezers, and then **remove** the skins. **Cut** the fillets in half lengthways and **roll** each one into a spiral shape.

Shave the carrots into thin strips. **Cut** the black radish into wafer-thin rounds.

Arrange three spirals of mackerel on each plate and **spoon** the lemon broth around. **Add** the carrot strips, chive flowers, black radish, purple cauliflower florets, and the herbs. Finally, **drizzle** with olive oil.

CHEF'S NOTE
The lemon broth will taste better if it is chilled. Place the broth on ice for a few minutes before serving. A perfect dish for summer.

BABY SQUID
STUFFED WITH
GOAT MILK
CHEESE

FARCIS À LA BROUSSE DU ROVE

Ingredients

8 totènes (small red
  squid from Marseille)
3 small bunches basil
1 small bunch cilantro
2 cups (1 lb. 2 oz./
  500 g) brousse du
  Rove (fresh, soft,
  goat milk curds)
1 lemon
5 black olives, pitted
  and sliced
Passedat olive oil*
Basil leaves, to garnish
Salt, pepper

Serves 4 | *Preparation time: 30 minutes* | *Cooking time: 6–7 minutes*

To clean the squid, **pull** the head and tentacles firmly away from the body with the innards and ink sac attached. **Cut off** the tentacles just below the eyes, **remove** the hard beak (mouth), reserving the tentacles. **Discard** the beak, head, and innards. **Pull out** the quill, **cut off** the fins, and discard. **Rinse** the tubes thoroughly under cold running water.

Wash the herbs, **remove** the stalks, and **chop** finely.

Put the soft cheese in a bowl and **add** the herbs. **Zest** the lemon into the bowl and **mix** in with a spatula. **Squeeze** the juice from the lemon and add. **Season** with salt and pepper to taste.

Spoon the mixture into a pastry bag fitted with a plain tip and **pipe** it into the squid tubes. **Close** the tubes with a toothpick. **Heat** water in a steamer to 150°F (70°C), **add** the squid and tentacles, and **steam** for 6–7 minutes.

Serve the squid in soup plates garnished with the olives and a drizzle of olive oil. **Shred** a few basil leaves and **scatter** over the dish along with some whole leaves.

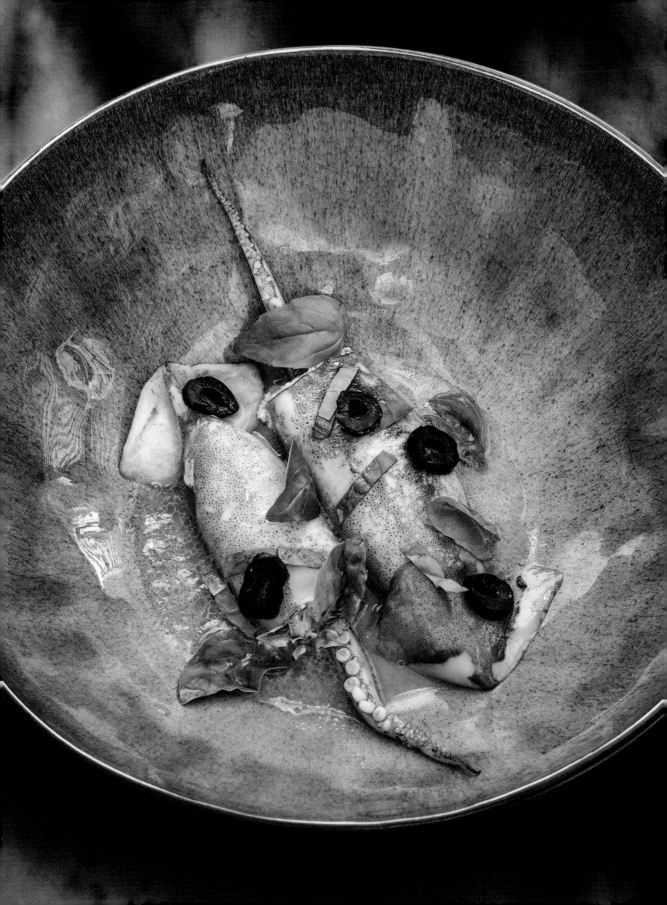

**Ingredients for scant
1 cup (7 oz./200 g)**

10 fully ripe plum
  tomatoes
3 cloves garlic
Scant ¾ cup (150 ml)
  Passedat olive oil*
1 sprig basil
1 sprig thyme
1 bay leaf
Salt, pepper

TOMATO SAUCE

Wash the tomatoes, **remove** the stalks, and **cut** a cross in the base of each one with a small knife to make them easier to peel. **Immerse** in boiling water for a few seconds, then in cold water; **slip off** the skins and **chop** them.

Preheat the oven to 300°F (150°C/Gas mark 2).

Peel the garlic and **chop** finely. **Put** the olive oil in an ovenproof dish and **place** in the oven to heat up. **Add** the garlic, chopped tomatoes, and herbs. **Cover** and **cook** in the oven for 2 hours.

Remove from the oven, **cool** slightly, then **put through** a food mill to reduce to a smooth purée. **Season** to taste.

T O M A T O E S
T H R E E
W A Y S

AUTOUR DE LA TOMATE

**Ingredients for
1 ¼ cups (7 oz./200 g)**

6 plum tomatoes
1 clove garlic
2 shallots
¼ cup (55 ml) Passedat
  olive oil*
1 sprig thyme
1 bay leaf
Salt, pepper

TOMATO CONCASSÉ

Wash the tomatoes, **remove** the stalks, and **cut** a cross in the base of each one with a small knife to make them easier to peel. **Immerse** in boiling water for a few seconds, then in cold water; **slip off** the skins. **Quarter** the tomatoes, **remove** the core and seeds, and discard. **Chop** the flesh into small cubes and **season** with salt and pepper.

Chop the garlic and shallots finely.

Heat the olive oil in a pan and **sweat** the garlic and shallots. **Add** the chopped tomatoes, thyme, and bay leaf. **Check** the seasoning and **cook** for an additional 2–3 minutes.

Ingredients for scant 1 cup (7 oz./200 g)

6 plum tomatoes
2 shallots
1 clove garlic
1 tablespoon mustard
Scant ½ cup (100 ml)
   sherry vinegar
Scant ¾ cup (150 ml)
   Passedat olive oil*
2 sprigs basil
Salt, pepper

TOMATO VINAIGRETTE

Peel the shallots and garlic. Roughly **chop** the shallots and tomatoes, then **crush** them with the garlic in a pestle and mortar. **Add** the mustard, vinegar, and olive oil. **Add** salt and pepper to taste.

Press the tomato mixture through a fine-mesh sieve using a small ladle. **Chop** the basil finely and **stir** into the mixture.

CHICKPEA, GRAPEFRUIT, AND HUMMUS SALAD

SALADE DE POIS CHICHE, PAMPLEMOUSSE ET HOUMOUS

Ingredients

1 lb. 2 oz. (500 g) chickpeas

1 lemon

1 teaspoon ground cumin

Passedat olive oil*

2 grapefruit

1 red onion

1 small bunch cilantro

1 tablespoon sunflower seeds

2 teaspoons (10 ml) sherry vinegar

1 teaspoon Passedat Curry Fakir* (curry powder)

Salt, pepper

Serves 4 | *Preparation time: 1 hour 15 minutes* | *Soaking time: overnight* | *Cooking time: 30 minutes*

Soak the chickpeas overnight in cold water. **Drain, place** in a saucepan, and **cover** with fresh water. **Bring to a boil** and **boil** for 30 minutes. **Drain** again, reserving the cooking water. **Divide** the chickpeas between two bowls.

Peel the zest from the lemon, **cut** into julienne strips, and **reserve**. **Juice** the lemon.

Put the chickpeas from one bowl in a food processor. **Add** the cumin and a little of the cooking water from the chickpeas and **grind** to a paste. **Add** lemon juice, salt and pepper, and enough olive oil to process to a smooth hummus. **Divide** the hummus between four individual serving bowls.

Peel the grapefruit and **divide** them into segments, removing all pith and membrane. **Cut** the segments into small pieces. **Peel** the onion and **chop** finely. **Remove** the stalks from the cilantro and **reserve** the leaves.

Add the grapefruit, sunflower seeds, vinegar, curry powder, cilantro leaves, and onion to the second bowl of chickpeas. **Moisten** with olive oil and **mix** all the ingredients together. **Add** salt and pepper to taste. **Place** in a serving dish and **garnish** with the lemon zest julienne.

"BOUILLE ABAISSE" TERRINE

TERRINE DE BOUILLE ABAISSE

Ingredients

1 lobster tail
1 bouquet garni
1 pinch saffron powder
1 ¾ cups (400 ml) fish
   stock
2 weever fish fillets
2 John Dory
   fillets, weighing
   approximately 7 oz.
   (200 g) each
1 beefsteak tomato
2 tablespoons (30 ml)
   Passedat olive oil*
2 potatoes
2 scallions
2 sticks celery
2 leaves gelatin
Salt, pepper

Serves 4 | *Preparation time: 2 hours* | *Cooking time: 45 minutes* | *Setting time: 6 hours*

Poach the lobster tail in simmering water with the bouquet garni for 4 minutes; **drain** and **allow to cool. Remove** the flesh from the shell and **chop** into pieces; **reserve.**

Add the saffron to the fish stock. **Poach** all the fish fillets in half of the fish stock for 10 minutes. **Season** with salt and pepper to taste and **allow to cool. Remove** the fillets from the stock and **set aside. Reserve** the stock.

Preheat oven to 300°F (150°C/Gas mark 2).

Wash and **slice** the tomato and **put** the slices in an ovenproof dish. **Add** the olive oil and **season** with salt and pepper. **Cook** in the oven for 15 minutes.

Peel and **slice** the potatoes and **cook** them in the reserved fish stock for approximately 15 minutes until tender.

Peel and **chop** the scallions finely, **blanch** them in boiling water, and **refresh** under cold running water. **Blanch** the celery sticks, **refresh**, and **cut** them into lengths the same size as the terrine dish.

Soak the gelatin in cold water to soften the leaves. **Heat** the remaining fish stock and **season** with salt and pepper. **Drain** the gelatin and **stir** the leaves into the stock until they dissolve.

When the stock begins to set and has reached the "wobbly" stage, **place** the fish fillets, tomatoes, potatoes, scallions, and celery in the terrine dish in alternate layers, placing the lobster pieces in the center. **Spoon** over the stock. **Cover** and **place** a weight on top, then **refrigerate** for approximately 6 hours or until set.

CHEF'S SALAD FROM LE PETIT NICE RESTAURANT

SALADE DU PETIT NICE

Ingredients

5 zucchini

Scant ¾ cup (150 ml)
  Passedat olive oil*

1 clove garlic

2 small red bell peppers

1 bulb fennel

1 small turnip

1 lettuce heart

1 celery heart

2 purple scallions

2 avocados

1 mango

2 oz. (50 g) horseradish
  root

2 tablespoons (30 ml)
  lemon juice

1 small bunch chervil

1 small bunch dill

Salt, pepper

Serves 4 | *Preparation time: 45 minutes* | *Cooking time: 2 hours 45 minutes*

Preheat the oven to 300°F (150°C/Gas mark 2).

Make a purée with three of the zucchini. **Wash**, **slice**, and **cook** them in a covered sauté pan with a splash of olive oil and the garlic. When cooked, **reduce** to a purée in a food processor and then **sieve** or **pass** them through a vegetable mill. **Add** salt and pepper to taste and **reserve**.

Clean the bell peppers and **roast** them in the oven for 2 ½ hours. **Take** them **out** of the oven, **remove** the skin, and **slice** into strips. **Heat** 3 tablespoons of olive oil in a skillet, **add** the sliced bell peppers, **season** with a pinch of salt, and **sauté** for 15 minutes. **Reserve**.

Wash the fennel, turnip, lettuce and celery hearts, and scallions. **Peel** the turnip. **Shave** the remaining zucchini into thin ribbons using a vegetable peeler, and **cut up** the rest of the vegetables carefully so they will look attractive on the serving dish. **Blanch** them in boiling water, **refresh** in iced water, and **reserve**.

Cut the avocados in half, **remove** the skin and pits, and **slice** them thickly. **Brush** them lightly with olive oil and season with salt and pepper. **Preheat** a ribbed grill pan and **color** the avocado briefly on both sides. **Reserve**.

Make a mango and horseradish vinaigrette. **Peel** the mango, **cut** the flesh away from the fibrous pit, and **chop** the flesh into small cubes. **Peel** the horseradish and **grate** on a microplane. **Put** the mango and horseradish in a small bowl, **add** the lemon juice and the remaining olive oil. **Season** with salt and pepper to taste.

Arrange the blanched vegetables and red bell pepper confit on a serving dish, **season** with salt and pepper, then **dress** with the vinaigrette. **Place** a mound of zucchini purée in the center and **lay** the avocado slices on top. **Garnish** with a few fronds of dill and chervil.

HEIRLOOM
TOMATO
AND STRAWBERRY
SALAD

TOMATES ANCIENNES ET FRAISES

Ingredients

8 heirloom tomatoes
   (pineapple, green
   zebra, beefsteak, etc.)
2 shallots
Scant ½ cup (100 ml)
   white Pineau des
   Charentes vinegar
1 cup (4 ¼ oz./125 g)
   Mara strawberries
   (cultivated woodland
   strawberries)
1 small bunch basil
1 small bunch purple
   basil
½ cup (110 ml)
   Passedat olive oil*
Fleur de sel de Camargue
   (Camargue sea salt)
Freshly ground black
   pepper

Serves 4 | *Preparation time: 25 minutes*

Wash the tomatoes, **remove** the stalks, and **cut** a cross in the base of each one with a small knife to make them easier to peel. **Immerse** in boiling water for a few seconds, then in cold water; **slip off** the skins and **reserve**.

Chop the shallots finely. **Place** them in a small pan with the vinegar and **cook** over a high heat until all the vinegar has evaporated. **Reserve.**

Wash the strawberries, **remove** their stalks, and **slice** them lengthways.

Wash both bunches of basil and **pick** the leaves off the stalks.

Slice the tomatoes thinly and **arrange** on a serving dish with the strawberry slices between them. **Sprinkle** over the shallots in vinegar and **drizzle** with the olive oil. **Season** with *fleur de sel* and freshly ground pepper, then **garnish** with the basil leaves.

CHEF'S NOTE

The sweetness of the strawberries marries perfectly with the acidity of the ripe, summer tomatoes in this salad.

MAIN
COURSES

SEA BREAM IN A GARLIC BOUILLON

AÏGO BOULIDO

Ingredients

4 small sea bream,
  weighing 12 oz.
  (350 g) each
3 heads garlic
6 shallots
2 cups (1 lb. 2 oz./
  500 g) kosher salt
2 cups (500 ml) fish
  stock
5 oz. (150 g) any white
  fish fillets
Scant ¼ cup (50 ml)
  whipping cream
6 sage leaves
Salt, pepper

Serves 4 | *Preparation time: 2 hours* | *Cooking time: 2 hours 15 minutes*

Preheat the oven to 300°F (150°C/Gas mark 2).

Put two of the heads of garlic and all the shallots between two layers of kosher salt in an ovenproof dish and **cook** in the oven for 1 hour 30 minutes. When cooked, **cut** the shallots in half lengthways and **squeeze** the soft garlic from the heads. **Set aside.**

Reduce the oven temperature to 250°F (130°C/Gas mark ½).

Clean and **scale** the four sea bream. **Remove** the two fillets from each fish by slicing lengthways along the backbone on either side, but leaving the fillets attached at the belly. **Clean** the fish, **remove** the bones and **skin,** and **lay** them side by side in an ovenproof dish. **Season, pour** over 1 cup (250 ml) of the stock, and **cook** in the oven for 15 minutes.

Remove any bones or pieces of skin from the white fish fillets, **put** the remaining stock in a saucepan, and **add** the fillets. **Separate** the third head of garlic into cloves, **peel** them, and **add** to the saucepan. **Cook** for 30 minutes. **Remove** the saucepan from the heat, **add** the cream and two sage leaves, and **allow to infuse** for a few minutes. **Remove** and discard the sage leaves. **Pour** this bouillon into a liquidizer and **blend** until smooth. **Add** salt and pepper to taste.

Pour a little bouillon into each soup plate and **lay** a sea bream fillet in the center. **Arrange** three shallot halves and a sage leaf around it, then **place** a quenelle-shaped teaspoonful of the reserved garlic purée on top.

S P I C E D
V E G E T A B L E
C O U S C O U S

C O U S C O U S   D E   L É G U M E S

Ingredients

½ cup (3 oz./80 g) chickpeas

1 lb. 5 oz. (600 g) beef trimmings

1 tablespoon (15 ml) Passedat olive oil*

1 bouquet garni

2 zucchini

1 large artichoke

½ red bell pepper

2 orange carrots

2 yellow carrots

1 small turnip

¾ cup (200 ml) concentrated chicken stock

3 tablespoons (1 oz./30 g) raisins

1 ½ tablespoons (½ oz./15 g) golden raisins

½ cup (2 ½ oz./80 g) couscous

1 orange

⅔ cup (150 ml) sheep milk

1 ⅓ tablespoons (⅓ oz./10 g) Passedat Volubilis Couscous spice mix*

Salt, pepper

Serves 4 | *Preparation time: 1 hour* | *Soaking time: overnight* | *Cooking time: 1 hour*

A day ahead, **soak** the chickpeas in a bowl of cold water. **Make** a concentrated beef *jus*. **Sauté** the beef trimmings in the olive oil, and **add** the bouquet garni and enough water to cover. **Bring** to a boil and **cook** until the liquid has reduced to 20 percent. **Strain** and **reserve** ¾ cup (200 ml).

The following day, **slice** one of the zucchini into rounds, **blanch** in boiling water, then **refresh** in iced water. **Drain**, **blend** to a purée in a food processor, and **add** salt and pepper to taste. **Remove** the outer leaves of the artichoke, **cut off** the top half, and then **scoop out** the inside leaves and the hairy choke. **Cut** the remaining heart into quarters. **Cook** in boiling water for 10 minutes, then **push** it through a fine-mesh sieve and **add** salt and pepper to taste. **Roast** the half bell pepper for 15 minutes on each side in a 300°F (150°C/ Gas mark 2) oven, **remove** the skin and seeds, and **slice** lengthways. **Peel** the carrots and turnip, **wash** the remaining zucchini, and **shape** them into small cylinders using an apple corer.

Mix together the beef *jus* and chicken stock in a saucepan, **season** with salt and pepper, and **place** over the heat. **Drain** the soaked chickpeas and **cook** them in the stock until tender. **Add** the cylinders of vegetables and **cook** them too, then **remove** the saucepan from the heat, **add** the raisins, and **leave** them to plump up.

Soak the couscous in a little water, a splash of olive oil, and a pinch of salt until the grains swell and absorb the water. **Reserve**. **Slice** the orange into rounds without peeling it, then lightly **brown** the slices on a preheated ribbed grill pan. **Warm** the sheep milk with the spice mix, then **process** in a blender or centrifuge to obtain a foam. **Warm through** all the prepared ingredients and **arrange** them attractively in a deep serving dish, with the vegetables on top of the zucchini and artichoke purées, and the foam poured over the top.

C H E F ' S   N O T E
Replace the meat stocks with vegetable stock for a vegetarian version.

PUFF PASTRY TOPPED WITH ANCHOVY BAYALDI

FEUILLETÉ BAYALDI ANCHOIS

Ingredients

7 oz. (200 g) sheet
    puff pastry
2 Bintje potatoes,
    or another waxy
    salad variety
1 eggplant
2 zucchini
2 pineapple tomatoes
2 onions
15 salted anchovy
    fillets
2–3 tablespoons
    (30–45 ml) milk
3 ½ oz. (100 g)
    candied or sun-dried
    tomatoes, thinly sliced
12 black olives
24 capers
2 cloves garlic
1 small bunch thyme
Scant ½ cup (100 ml)
    Passedat olive oil*
Salt, pepper

Serves 4 | *Preparation time: 1 hour 30 minutes* | *Cooking time: 40 minutes*

Preheat the oven to 375°F (190°C/Gas mark 5). **Line** a baking sheet with parchment paper and **lay** the sheet of puff pastry on it. **Place** a wire cake rack on top and **bake** for 20 minutes. **Remove** the rack and **allow** the pastry to cool.

Slice all the vegetables into rounds ⅛ in. (3 mm) thick using a mandolin. **Soak** the anchovies in the milk to remove the salt and then **drain**. **Lower** the oven temperature to 325°F (170°C/Gas mark 3).

Arrange the vegetable slices in overlapping rows over the baked pastry. **Season** with salt and pepper, then **drizzle** with olive oil. **Arrange** the anchovies, candied or sun-dried tomatoes, olives, and capers in overlapping rows between the vegetables. **Chop** the garlic finely, **remove** the thyme leaves from their stalks, and **sprinkle** both on top. **Return** to the oven for 20 minutes.

CHEF'S NOTE

The version of this recipe without pastry is known as a vegetable tian— the name for a Provençal earthenware dish.

BOUILLE
ABAISSE

For me, the name of this dish—so emblematic of the cuisine of Marseille—is in two words, not one, as attests the preparation in two steps: "quand ça bout, tu (a)baisses le feu" (when it boils, you lower the heat). When making this soup, it's important not to boil the fish for too long or it will disintegrate and its flavor will be ruined.

Ingredients

1 weever fish, weighing 7 oz. (200 g)

1 monkfish tail, weighing 14 oz. (400 g)

1 Mediterranean scorpion fish

1 barracuda fish steak, weighing 7 oz. (200 g)

1 bœuf (Mediterranean fish)

8 freshwater tetra (galactic) fish

8 squill fish (mantis shrimps)

2 small spiny lobsters

3 plum tomatoes

4 potatoes

1 orange

3 cloves garlic

2 shallots

⅔ cup (150 ml) Passedat olive oil*

4 star anise

1 pinch fennel seeds

1 sprig thyme

2 bay leaves

4 cups (1 liter) fish stock

1 pinch saffron powder

1 pinch saffron threads

Salt, pepper

Serves 4 | *Preparation time: 1 hour 30 minutes* | *Cooking time: 35 minutes*

Clean all the fish, cutting off the heads and tails where necessary. **Cut** down through the bones, on the diagonal, dividing the fish into large pieces. **Leave** the barracuda steak whole; **cut** the crustaceans in half. **Reserve** them all in the refrigerator.

Wash the tomatoes, **remove** the stalks, and **cut** a cross in the base of each one with a small knife to make them easier to peel. **Immerse** in boiling water for a few seconds, then in cold water, and **slip off** the skins. **Quarter** the tomatoes, **remove** the core and seeds, and discard. **Chop** the flesh into small cubes and **season** with salt and pepper.

Peel the potatoes, **slice** into rounds, and **reserve**. Peel a thin strip of zest from the orange with the potato peeler.

Peel the garlic and the shallots, **chop** finely, and **sweat** them in a skillet with the olive oil. **Add** the potatoes, star anise, fennel seeds, thyme, and bay leaves, and **pour** in the stock. Finally **add** the diced tomato, saffron powder, and orange zest, and **crumble** in the saffron threads. **Season** lightly with salt and pepper. **Cook** this bouillon on a low heat for approximately 20 minutes.

Add the fish and **allow to cook** for approximately 20 minutes on a low heat.

At the same time, **cook** the crustaceans. **Brush** them with olive oil and **season** with salt and pepper, then **place** shell side down on a preheated grill pan, covering the pan if possible. Once the flesh has turned opaque, **remove** the grill pan from the heat.

Arrange all the fish and crustaceans on a serving platter and **pour** a generous quantity of the bouillon around them.

CHEF'S NOTE

If some of the fish used in this recipe are unavailable, choose a selection of different fish and shellfish according to what is locally available.

MARSEILLE-STYLE FISH BALLS

BOULETTES DE POISSON À LA MARSEILLAISE

Ingredients

1 lb. 5 oz. (600 g)
  white fish fillets
  (e.g. monkfish, turbot,
  or sea bream)
1 preserved lemon
  in salt
1 small bunch cilantro
1 ½ oz. (40 g) sun-dried
  tomatoes
1 small bunch chives
2 shallots
Passedat olive oil*
1 teaspoon ground
  cumin
1 teaspoon ground
  turmeric
2 eggs
Scant ½ cup (50 g)
  all-purpose flour
3 ⅓ cups (7 oz./200 g)
  fresh bread crumbs
2 bulbs fennel with
  leafy tops
14 oz. (400 g) potatoes
1 onion
2 cloves garlic
1 pinch saffron powder
1 star anise
8 cups (2 liters) fish
  stock
Salt, pepper

Serves 4 | *Preparation time: 2 hours* | *Cooking time: 1 hour*

Remove any bones or remaining skin from the fish fillets. **Cut** them into small cubes and **reserve**.

Rinse the salt from the preserved lemon, **cut** in half, **remove** the pulp, and discard. **Chop** the cilantro, lemon rind, sun-dried tomatoes, and chives and **reserve**.

Peel the shallots, **chop** them finely, and **sweat** in a splash of olive oil in a skillet.

Mix them with the other chopped ingredients in a large bowl and **add** the cubes of fish, the ground spices, and the eggs. **Season** with salt and pepper. **Mix** everything together well.

Shape the mixture into small balls and **roll** them in the flour, then the bread crumbs until coated. **Place** on a baking sheet.

Trim the leafy fronds from the fennel bulbs and **reserve** for garnishing the dish. **Cut** the fennel bulbs and potatoes into small cubes of approximately ½ in. (1 cm). **Peel** and **chop** the onion and garlic.

Make a bouillon. **Sweat** all the chopped vegetables in a deep saucepan with a splash of olive oil. **Add** the saffron, star anise, and fish stock and **simmer** over a low heat for 45 minutes.

Preheat the oven to 325°F (160°C/Gas mark 3). **Drizzle** the fish balls with a little olive oil and **sprinkle** with salt and pepper. **Bake** for 15 minutes.

Arrange the fish balls in a deep serving dish, **pour** the bouillon around them, and **garnish** with the reserved fennel fronds.

SHOULDER OF LAMB BAKED IN HAY, WITH ASPARAGUS

ÉPAULE CUITE AU FOIN ET ASPERGES

Ingredients

1 shoulder of lamb,
    weighing 1 lb. 12 oz.
    (800 g)
2 cloves garlic
Groundnut oil
1 teaspoon butter
2 handfuls hay
3 ½ oz. (100 g) fresh
    peas, in the pod
7 oz. (200 g) fava beans,
    in the pod
2 oz. (50 g) green
    beans
1 bunch green
    asparagus
1 bunch scallions
Passedat olive oil*
Salt, pepper

Serves 4 | *Preparation time: 1 hour 30 minutes* | *Cooking time: 45 minutes*

Preheat the oven to 350°F (180°C/Gas mark 4).

Peel the garlic and **cut** into slivers. **Make** several small cuts with the point of a sharp knife in the skin of the lamb and **insert** the slivers of garlic.

Put the groundnut oil and butter in a large skillet, **place** over medium heat, and **brown** the lamb on both sides.

Put the hay and a little water in a casserole large enough to contain the lamb, **lay** the joint on the hay, **cover**, and **bake** for 20 minutes. **Remove** from the oven and **let rest** for 20 minutes.

While the lamb is cooking, **shell** the peas and fava beans, **top and tail** the green beans. **Cook** them in salted boiling water, then **drain** under cold running water.

Peel the asparagus and the scallions, then **put** them in a bowl, **add** a splash of oil, and **season** with salt and pepper. **Grill** them on a preheated ribbed grill pan.

Heat all the vegetables through together in a skillet with a splash of olive oil and a little water, **season** with salt and pepper. **Serve** with the lamb.

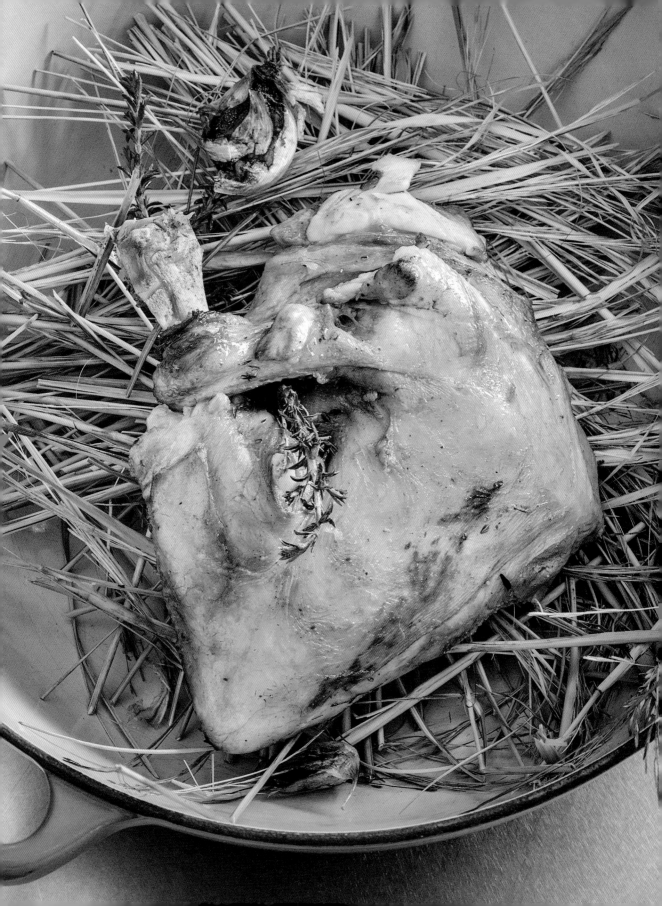

MARSEILLE-STYLE MONKFISH BOUILLON

BOUILLON DE PÊCHE À LA MARSEILLAISE

Ingredients

For the rouille

2 tomatoes, halved

1 tablespoon tomato paste

½ clove garlic

1 chili, chopped

(Alternatively, use a ready-made rouille sauce)

For the bouillon

1 monkfish tail, weighing 1 lb. 12 oz. (800 g)

1 ¼ cups (300 ml) water

1 sachet Passedat Tramontane bouillon*

1 yellow carrot

1 orange carrot

1 scallion

Passedat olive oil*

1 ¼ cups (300 ml) fish stock

2 tablespoons (1 oz./30 g) rouille

Espelette chili powder

1 small bunch hyssop

Salt, pepper

Serves 4 | *Preparation time: 3 hours 30 minutes* | *Infusing time: 20 minutes* | *Cooking time: 30 minutes*

To make the rouille, **preheat** the oven to 250°F (120°C/Gas mark ½). **Put** the tomato halves on a baking sheet with the tomato paste, garlic, and chili. **Season** with salt and pepper and **cook** in the oven for 2 hours, then **pass through** a fine-mesh sieve. **Reserve**.

To make the bouillon, **bring** the water **to a boil** and **add** the sachet of bouillon. **Cover**, remove from the heat, and **allow to infuse** for 20 minutes.

Peel the carrots and **cut** them into rounds. **Blanch** in boiling water until just tender, **drain**, and **refresh** under cold running water. **Reserve**.

Peel the scallion and **cut** into quarters. **Blanch** in boiling water, then **drain** and **refresh** under cold running water. **Dry** on paper towel. Lightly **oil** a ribbed grill pan and **grill** the scallion. **Reserve**.

Cut the monkfish tail into medallions and **poach** them in the fish stock for approximately 10 minutes. **Drain** and **arrange** them in soup plates with the carrots and scallions, then **pour** the hot bouillon around them and **garnish** with dots of the rouille.

Sprinkle over a little Espelette chili powder and garnish with a few sprigs of hyssop.

BEEF-FILLED SQUID IN TOMATO SAUCE

ENCORNETS FARCIS AU BOEUF
ET SAUCE TOMATE

Ingredients

2 large squid

1 shallot

1 clove garlic

Passedat olive oil*

1 oz. (30 g) sun-dried
tomatoes

1 small bunch parsley

2 oz. (50 g) sliced
white bread, crusts
removed

⅔ cup (150 ml) milk

10 oz. (300 g) ground
beef

1 sprig thyme

1 egg, beaten

1 ½ cups (10 oz./
300 g) tomato sauce
(see Tomatoes Three
Ways, p. 56)

1 sprig rosemary, plus
extra to garnish

Salt, pepper

Serves 4 | *Preparation time: 2 hours* | *Cooking time: 30 minutes*

Preheat the oven to 325°F (170°C/Gas mark 3).

To clean the squid, **pull** the head and tentacles firmly away from the body; the innards containing the ink sac will be attached. **Cut off** the tentacles just below the eyes, **remove** the hard beak (mouth), reserving the tentacles. **Discard** the beak, head, innards, and ink sac. **Pull out** the quill, **cut off** the fins and discard. **Rinse** the tubes thoroughly under running water.

Peel the shallot and garlic, **chop** the shallot, **crush** the garlic, and **put** them both in a skillet to sweat in a splash of olive oil. **Cut** the sun-dried tomatoes into small pieces and **add**.

Remove the stalks from the parsley and **chop** the leaves. **Soak** the bread in the milk for a few minutes, then **remove** and **squeeze out** the excess moisture. **Crumble** the bread into small pieces.

Put the ground beef in a large bowl and **add** the cooked shallot and garlic, the parsley, thyme leaves, crumbled bread, and egg. **Season** with salt and pepper and **mix** well. **Fill** the squid tubes with this stuffing.

Heat a tablespoon of olive oil in a skillet and lightly **brown** the squid tubes. **Transfer** to an ovenproof dish, **coat** with the tomato sauce, **add** the rosemary, and **cook** in the oven for 25 minutes.

Remove the squid from the dish and **cut** into slices. **Arrange** the slices overlapping on the tomato sauce. To serve, **garnish** with extra rosemary sprigs.

CHEF'S NOTE
Originally from Italy, this dish is also popular in the Endoume area of Marseille.

GNOCCHI WITH CREAMY HERB SAUCE

GNOCCHI AU JUS VERT

Ingredients

2 small bunches basil

2 small bunches parsley

2 ⅓ cups (1 lb. 2 oz./ 500 g) mashed potato

1 ¾ cups (6 ½ oz./180 g) white bread flour

1 egg yolk

Passedat olive oil*

1 head new season's garlic

2 tablespoons (30 ml) whipping cream

A few Parmesan shavings

1 tablespoon ricotta

Salt, pepper

Serves 4 | *Preparation time: 45 minutes* | *Cooking time: 2 minutes*

Wash the bunches of basil and parsley, reserving a few basil leaves for garnishing. **Blanch** together in boiling water and **refresh** under cold running water. **Shake off** excess water and **purée** the herbs in a food processor. **Pass through** a fine-mesh sieve.

Mix the mashed potato with the flour and the egg yolk, and **add** a little of the puréed herbs to make a dough firm enough to shape.

Shape the dough into several long rolls ¾ in. (2 cm) in diameter, and **cut** the rolls into ⅔ in. (1.5 cm) lengths with a knife. **Lay** them on parchment paper sprinkled with flour and **cover** with a damp cloth.

Break up the garlic into separate cloves, **peel** them and then **sweat** in a skillet in a splash of olive oil until soft. **Add** the remaining herb purée and **thin down** with the cream.

Plunge the gnocchi into a large pan of simmering water and **lift** them **out** with a slotted spoon as soon as they float to the surface. **Add** them to the skillet, **stir** into the sauce, and **check** the seasoning.

Serve in warmed soup plates, garnished with the reserved basil leaves, Parmesan shavings, and the ricotta.

GNOCCHETTI
WITH
TELLINS

GNOCCHETTI AUX TELLINES

Ingredients

1 lb. 5 oz. (600 g) tellins,
   or use cockles
14 oz. (400 g)
   gnocchetti pasta
   shells
1 small bunch parsley
1 shallot
Passedat olive oil*
½ glass dry white wine
1 cup (7 oz./200 g)
   tomato concassé
   (see Tomatoes Three
   Ways, p. 56)
Salt, pepper

Serves 4 | *Preparation time: 30 minutes* | *Soaking time: 12 hours* | *Cooking time: 15 minutes*

Soak the tellins for half a day in plenty of cold water to extract the sand, changing the water regularly.

Cook the pasta shells in boiling water for 10 minutes.

Remove the stalks from the parsley, and **reserve**. **Chop** the leaves and **reserve** them separately.

Peel and **chop** the shallot and **sweat** in a splash of olive oil in a deep pan. **Deglaze** with the white wine, then **boil** to reduce and **add** the tellins and the parsley stalks.

Place over a medium heat, **cover** the pan, and **cook** until all the tellins have opened.

Remove the parsley stalks, then **add** the pasta shells to the pan with the tomato concassé. **Season** to taste with salt, pepper, and olive oil just before serving and **sprinkle** with the chopped parsley leaves.

MY SUNDAY NIGHT PIZZA

MA PIZZA DU DIMANCHE SOIR

Ingredients

6 fresh anchovies
1 cup (9 oz./250 g)
   kosher salt
8 black olives
3 cloves garlic
10 ripe plum tomatoes
Scant ½ cup (100 ml)
   Passedat olive oil*
2 sprigs basil
9 oz. (250 g) bread
   dough, homemade
   or store bought
Flour
1 sprig thyme
Salt, pepper

Serves 4 | *Preparation time: 2 hours* | *Soaking time: 24 hours* |
Resting time: 1 hour | *Cooking time: 2 hours 10 minutes*

Remove the heads and **clean** the anchovies. To do this, **detach** the head with your fingers and **pull away** what comes with it. (Do not rinse the anchovies in water.)

Fillet the anchovies. **Place** half the kosher salt on a large plate, **lay** the fillets on top in a single layer, and **cover** with the remaining salt. **Leave** for 24 hours in a cool place.

Remove the pits from the olives, **chop** them finely, **place** them on paper towel, and **leave** them to dry out in a warm, dry place for half a day.

Make the tomato sauce. **Peel** and **crush** the garlic, roughly **chop** five of the tomatoes. **Put** a splash of olive oil in a skillet and **add** the garlic, tomatoes, and one sprig of the basil. **Season** with salt and pepper, **cover** the pan, and **cook** over low heat for 2 hours. **Pass** through a food mill. **Cool**.

Roll out the bread dough thinly into a large round on a sheet of parchment paper. **Sprinkle** with flour and **let rest** on the parchment paper for at least an hour, covered with a cloth to prevent the dough drying out.

At the same time, **soak** the salted anchovy fillets in cold water for 1 hour, **drain**, then **cut** them in half lengthways and **reserve** in a cool place.

Remove the stalk from the thyme and roughly **chop** the leaves. **Preheat** the oven to 425°F (220°C/Gas mark 7).

Spread the tomato sauce over the rolled-out dough, **slice** the remaining five tomatoes and the garlic finely, and **lay** them on top. **Arrange** the anchovy fillets over the tomatoes and garlic and **sprinkle** with the dried olives and thyme leaves.

Bake the pizza for approximately 10 minutes. **Drizzle** with olive oil, **chop** the leaves from the remaining basil sprig, and **sprinkle** over before serving.

ROASTED RED MULLET WITH THYME AND MARSEILLE BELL PEPPERS

ROUGETS RÔTIS AU THYM, POIVRONS MARSEILLAIS

Ingredients

2 large red mullet,
   weighing 1 lb. 5 oz.
   (600 g) each
4 small, green Marseille
   bell peppers
Passedat olive oil*
1 small bunch thyme
8 sprigs fennel
2 green tomatoes
1 head new season's
   garlic
15 black olives
1 tablespoon (20 g)
   capers
Fleur de sel, pepper

Serves 4 | *Preparation time: 45 minutes* | *Cooking time: 25 minutes*

Descale the red mullet, **clean** and **cut off** the heads. **Rinse** well in cold water.

Preheat the oven to 350°F (180°C/Gas mark 4).

Preheat a ribbed grill pan and **grill** the bell peppers on all sides. **Transfer** the grill pan to the oven for 10 minutes to finish cooking the peppers. **Remove** and **keep warm. Lower** the oven temperature to 325°F (160°C/Gas mark 3).

Brush a baking sheet with olive oil, **sprinkle** it with *fleur de sel* and pepper, and **lay** the red mullet on it. **Make** a few small slits in the skin and **insert** little sprigs of thyme in them. **Tuck** the sprigs of fennel into the belly cavities.

Slice the green tomatoes into rounds. **Cut** the head of garlic in half and **place** around the fish with the sliced tomatoes. **Sprinkle** with the black olives and capers and **bake** for 15 minutes.

Arrange the bell peppers around the fish before serving.

CAMARGUE BLACK RICE PAELLA

PAËLLA AU RIZ NOIR DE CAMARGUE

Ingredients

2 cups (10 oz./300 g) black rice from the Camargue

¼ cup (50 ml) Passedat olive oil*

1 shallot

2 bay leaves

2 sprigs thyme

2 scant cups (450 ml) fish stock

24 carpet-shell clams

¼ cup (50 ml) dry white wine

2 cuttlefish, weighing 14 oz. (400 g) each

1 pinch saffron threads

Salt, pepper

Serves 4 | *Preparation time: 1 hour 30 minutes* | *Soaking time: 48 hours* | *Cooking time: 30 minutes*

Soak the rice in cold water for 48 hours before you begin cooking the paella.

Drain the rice thoroughly. **Preheat** the oven to 400°F (200°C/Gas mark 6).

Heat half of the olive oil in a large flameproof pan, **add** the shallot, one bay leaf, and a sprig of thyme. **Add** the rice and **toast** it by stirring the grains vigorously around the bottom of the casserole over the heat. **Season** with salt and **add** the fish stock. **Cover** and **transfer** the pan to the oven; **cook** for approximately 20 minutes.

Soak the clams in cold water for 30 minutes to extract any sand. **Cook** them in a covered pan with the white wine, and the remaining bay leaf and thyme. When cooked, **shell**, and **reserve** their juice.

Clean the cuttlefish. **Pull** the head and tentacles firmly away from the body; the innards containing the ink sac will be attached. **Cut off** the tentacles just below the eyes, **cut** them into short lengths, and **reserve**. **Discard** the head and innards. **Pull out** the quill and discard and then **rinse** the tubes thoroughly under cold running water. **Remove** the outer membrane and fins and **cut** the cuttlefish into strips.

Sauté the tentacles and the strips briefly on both sides in a skillet with the remaining olive oil, and **season** with salt and pepper.

Add the cuttlefish to the rice and **crumble** over the saffron threads. **Add** the clams with their juice just before serving.

CHEF'S NOTE

There are other varieties of Camargue rice, such as red rice, that you can enjoy experimenting with.

RATATOUILLE
MY WAY

Ingredients

7 oz. (200 g) puff
   pastry, ready
   prepared
4 white onions
⅔ cup (150 ml)
   Passedat olive oil*
2 red bell peppers
5 plum tomatoes
2 eggplants
3 zucchini
4 bay leaves
2 sprigs basil
2 sprigs thyme
Salt, pepper

Serves 4 | *Preparation time: 1 hour 30 minutes* | *Cooking time: 2 hours 45 minutes*

Preheat the oven to 350°F (180°C/Gas mark 4).

Roll out the puff pastry thinly into a rectangle about ⅛ in. (3 mm) thick. **Drape** the pastry over the rolling pin and **unroll** it onto a baking sheet. **Place** a wire cake rack on top and **bake** the pastry for about 15 minutes or until golden brown. **Allow to cool** a little, then **cut** into four 4 in. (10 cm) rounds using a plain pastry cutter.

Peel and finely **chop** the onions and **sweat** them in a pan in a little olive oil. **Season** with salt and pepper and then **cover** the pan and **stew** the onions for 45 minutes. **Drain** through a sieve to remove excess oil. **Reserve**.

Preheat the oven to 300°F (150°C/Gas mark 2). **Wash** all the remaining vegetables. **Brush** the bell peppers with olive oil and **season**. **Lay** on a baking sheet and **cook** in the oven for 1 hour.

Meanwhile, **remove** the stalks from the tomatoes and **cut** a cross with a small knife in the base of each tomato to make them easier to peel. **Immerse** in boiling water for a few seconds and then in cold water. **Slip off** the skins, **quarter** the tomatoes, **remove** the cores and seeds, and discard. **Oil** a baking sheet and **lay** the tomato quarters on it.

Slice the eggplant and zucchini lengthways, leaving the skin on. **Add** the slices to the baking sheet with the tomatoes on it, spreading the vegetables out in a single layer. **Season** with salt and pepper and **cook** in the oven for 45 minutes.

When the vegetables are cooked, **cut** them into even-sized rounds using a 1 in. (2.5 cm) plain pastry cutter. **Spread** the stewed onions over the pastry rounds and **arrange** the vegetables in overlapping rings on top. **Make** small bouquets with a few sprigs of basil and thyme and **place** in the center of the ratatouille "galettes." **Serve** cold and **drizzle** with olive oil just before serving.

MY
FISH
&
CHIPS

Ingredients

14 oz. (400 g) white
  fish fillets (e.g. sea
  bream, cod)
1 lemon
1 ½ cups (5 ¼ oz./
  150 g) tempura (or
  all-purpose) flour
¾ cup (180 ml) water
⅓ cup (1 ¾ oz./50 g)
  white sesame seeds
2 Bintje potatoes,
  or another waxy
  salad variety
4 cups (1 liter)
  grapeseed oil,
  for deep frying
Salt, pepper

For the green sauce

5 oz. (150 g) zucchini
¼ oz. (7 g) garlic
⅔ oz. (20 g) chives
½ oz. (15 g) tarragon
½ oz. (15 g) cilantro
Generous ½ cup
  (5 oz./150g) plain
  yogurt

Serves 4 | *Preparation time: 1 hour* | *Cooking time: 10 minutes*

Cut the fish fillets into rectangles measuring 4 x ¾ in. (10 x 2 cm) and **reserve** in the refrigerator.

Zest the lemon and **squeeze** the juice. **Mix** the tempura flour with the water to make a smooth batter, **add** the lemon zest and sesame seeds.

Wash and **peel** the potatoes, **slice** them thinly on a mandolin. **Reserve** them in a bowl of cold water.

Make the green sauce. **Wash** the zucchini and **cut** them into rounds. **Blanch** them in boiling water, then **refresh** under cold running water and **drain** well.

Peel the garlic cloves and **wash** all the herbs. **Put** them into a food processor with the zucchini and the yogurt. **Reduce** to a purée and **push through** a fine-mesh sieve. **Add** salt and pepper to taste and **reserve**.

Heat the oil to 340°F (170°C) in a deep pan. Using tongs, **dip** the rectangles of fish in the tempura batter to coat them, then **fry** them, a few at a time, in the hot oil. **Remove** with a slotted spoon and **allow to drain** on a plate lined with paper towel. **Season** with salt and lemon juice.

Next, **fry** the potato slices and **drain** them on a plate lined with paper towel. **Season**.

Serve immediately accompanied by the green sauce.

AUNT GUITE'S LITTLE PROVENÇAL STUFFED VEGETABLES

PETITS FARCIS PROVENÇAUX DE TANTE GUITE

Ingredients

4 small round turnips
2 zucchini
3 tomatoes
4 white button
    mushrooms
1 eggplant
2 onions
1 sprig thyme
1 ¾ cups (400 ml)
    beef stock
Salt, pepper

For the stuffing

3 shallots
2 cloves garlic
Passedat olive oil*
7 oz. (200 g) white
    bread, crusts
    removed
2 cups (500 ml) milk
1 small bunch parsley
14 oz. (400 g) ground
    beef
3 ½ oz. (100 g) sausage
    meat
1 egg, beaten

Serves 4 | *Preparation time: 2 hours* | *Cooking time: 1 hour*

Wash all the vegetables and **cut** them into even-sized pieces. **Scoop** a hollow out of each one, using a melon baller, to hold the stuffing.

Make the stuffing. **Peel** and finely **chop** the shallots and garlic and **sweat** them until lightly browned in a skillet with a splash of olive oil.

Soak the bread in the milk for a few minutes and then **squeeze out** the excess moisture. **Crumble** into small pieces. **Remove** the leaves from the parsley stalks and **chop** them.

Mix the shallots, garlic, crumbled bread, and chopped parsley leaves together in a large bowl. **Stir** in the ground beef, breaking up any lumps of meat with the spoon, the sausage meat, and the egg. **Season** with salt and pepper.

Preheat the oven to 350°F (180°C/Gas mark 4).

Remove the leaves from the thyme and **chop** them. **Fill** the hollows in the vegetables with the stuffing. **Arrange** the vegetables side by side in an ovenproof dish, **sprinkle** with the thyme, and **pour** over the beef stock. **Cook** in the oven for 1 hour, basting the vegetables regularly with the stock.

UNCLE JÉSUS'S SPIDER CRAB SOUP

SOUPE D'ESQUINADE DE JÉSUS

Ingredients

1 spider crab
(esquinade), weighing
approximately
2 lb. 4 oz. (1 kg),
with its eggs
1 bouquet garni made
up of leek, thyme,
parsley, bay leaf
1 shallot
2 cloves garlic
¼ cup (50 ml) Passedat
olive oil*
1 sprig thyme
2 cups (500 ml) fish
stock
Salt, pepper

Serves 4 | *Preparation time: 1 hour* | *Cooking time: 15 minutes*

Kill the crab by making an incision in its head with a sharp knife, or get the fishmonger to do this for you.

Remove the claws and **blanch** them in a court bouillon to cover with the bouquet garni for 2 minutes. **Shell** the claws and **reserve** the meat.

Take off the carapace and **remove** the coral; **reserve** in the refrigerator. **Wash** the carapace and **reserve**.

Break up the body of the crab with a heavy knife. **Peel** and **chop** the shallot and **crush** the garlic without peeling it.

Sauté the pieces of crab in a pan in the olive oil with the shallot and garlic, **add** the thyme and the fish stock, and **cook** until the liquid has reduced by half. **Process** in a centrifuge or food processor, then **strain** through a fine-mesh sieve and **mix** in the coral. **Check** the seasoning and **adjust** if necessary.

Lightly **sauté** the crab eggs in a pan in a little olive oil. Using a small plain pastry cutter as a mold, **create** a disc of crab claw meat and **cover** the top with the eggs. **Put** the carapace in a dish, then place the disc in the center and **pour** the bisque around it.

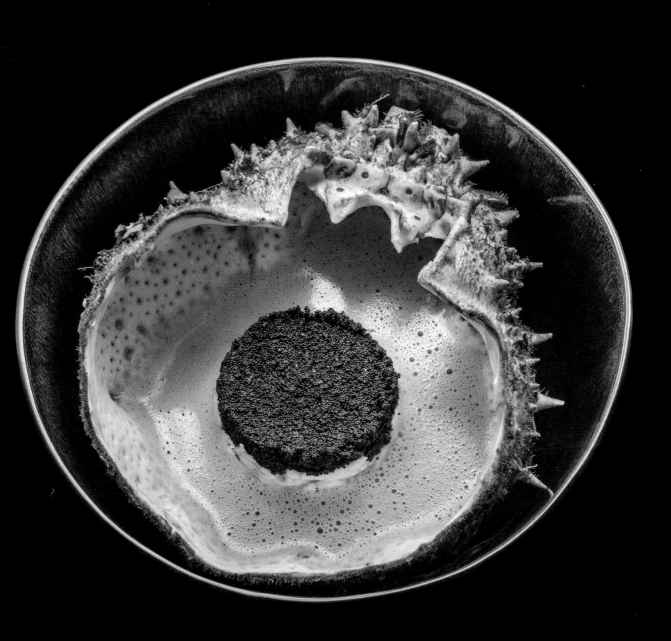

GRANDFATHER BARTHÉLEMY'S PISTOU SOUP

SOUPE AU PISTOU BARTHÉLEMY

Ingredients

½ cup (3 ½ oz./100 g) dried borlotti beans
2 potatoes
2 zucchini
3 ½ oz. (100 g) green beans
3 ½ oz. (100 g) flat green beans
2 plum tomatoes
½ cup (3 ½ oz./100 g) navy (haricot) beans (preferably coco)
1 ¼ cups (5 oz./150 g) elbow pasta (macaroni) or other small pasta shapes
Salt, pepper

For the pistou
3 cloves garlic
1 small bunch basil
¼ cup (1 ½ oz./40 g) grated Parmesan
3 ½ tablespoons (1 oz./30 g) pine nuts
Scant ½ cup (100 ml) Passedat olive oil*

Serves 4 | *Preparation time: 1 hour 30 minutes* | *Soaking time: 12 hours* | *Cooking time: 50 minutes*

Soak the borlotti beans in cold water for 12 hours before making the soup.

Wash all the vegetables. **Peel** the potatoes and **cut** them into approximately ½ in. (1 cm) cubes. **Cut** the zucchini into cubes of the same size. **Cut** the green beans and flat beans into lengths of approximately ½ in. (1 cm). **Reserve** the prepared vegetables.

Remove the stalks from the tomatoes and **cut** a cross in the base of each one with a small knife to make them easier to peel. **Immerse** in boiling water for a few seconds, then in cold water and **slip off** the skins. **Quarter** the tomatoes, **remove** the cores, and **scoop out** the pulp. **Chop** the tomato flesh into small cubes and **reserve**.

Drain the borlotti beans and **put** in a large pan of cold water with the navy beans. **Place** on the heat and **cook** for 20 minutes. **Add** the potatoes, zucchini, green beans, and flat beans and **let cook** for an additional 20 minutes. **Add** the pasta and **cook** for an additional 10 minutes.

Make the pistou. **Peel** the garlic, **remove** the stalks from the basil, and **put** the leaves in a mortar with the garlic, Parmesan, and pine nuts. **Grind** with the pestle, gradually adding the olive oil until you have a smooth, thick pistou sauce. **Season** with salt and pepper to taste.

Take the soup off the heat and **add** the pistou, **check** the seasoning, and **serve** hot.

SPELT TABBOULEH WITH MUSSELS, RAISINS, AND MINT

TABOULÉ D'ÉPEAUTRE AUX MOULES, RAISINS SECS ET MENTHE

Ingredients

2 cups (7 oz./200 g) spelt

1 lb. 5 oz. (600 g) fresh mussels in the shell

2 tablespoons (⅔ oz./20 g) raisins

1 cucumber

1 lemon

2 shallots

1 small bunch parsley

1 small bunch mint

4 teaspoons (20 ml) Passedat olive oil*

Salt, pepper

For the marinière (for cooking the mussels)

1 small bunch thyme

1 onion

⅓ cup (75 ml) dry white wine

Serves 4 | *Preparation time: 45 minutes* | *Chilling time: 1 hour* | *Cooking time: 15 minutes*

Put the spelt in a pan with cold water to cover and bring to a boil. **Cook** for 15 minutes. **Drain, allow to cool,** and **reserve.**

Rinse the mussels thoroughly under cold running water. **Discard** any that are open but do not close when their shells are firmly tapped.

Make the *marinière*. **Wash** the bunch of thyme. **Peel** and **slice** the onion and **put** it in a large pan with the wine and thyme. **Place** the mussels on top, **cover** the pan, and **set** over a high heat. When all the mussels have opened, **remove** from the heat. **Shell** the mussels, **allow to cool,** and **reserve** the mussel meat in the refrigerator when cooled.

Soak the raisins in warm water to cover. **Peel** the cucumber, **cut** in two lengthways, **scoop out** the seeds, and **cut** the flesh into small cubes. **Juice** the lemon and **peel** and **chop** the shallots finely.

Remove the stalks from the parsley and mint and roughly **chop** all the leaves together. **Drain** the raisins.

Put the spelt and the mussels in a large bowl and **add** the cucumber, raisins, herbs, and shallot. **Season** with the lemon juice, olive oil, salt, and pepper to taste. Carefully **stir** all the ingredients together with a large spoon and **chill** for 1 hour before serving.

RED
ONION
PISSALADIÈRE

PISSALADIÈRE AUX OIGNONS ROUGES

Ingredients

7 oz. (200 g) bread
  dough, ready
  prepared
Flour
1 egg yolk
3 red onions
Scant ½ cup (100 ml)
  Passedat olive oil*
8 anchovy fillets in salt
1 sprig summer savory
10 Niçoise (small, black)
  olives
Salt, pepper

Serves 4 | *Preparation time: 2 hours* | *Resting time: 1 hour* | *Cooking time: 1 hour 40 minutes*

Reserve a quarter of the dough. Using a rolling pin, **roll out** the remainder thinly on a board lightly dusted with flour into an oval shape. **Lift** onto a baking sheet. **Cut** the reserved piece of dough in half and, with the palms of your hands, **roll** each piece into a long, thin sausage shape. **Twist** the two together to form a braid.

Brush the edges of the rolled-out dough with the egg yolk and **press** the braid firmly around it. **Brush** the braid with the remaining egg yolk. **Sprinkle** the dough with a little flour, **cover** with a cloth to prevent it drying out, and **allow to rest** for 1 hour.

Peel and finely **chop** the red onions. **Stew** them in a covered pan with most of the olive oil, leaving a little for serving, for 1 hour 30 minutes over a low heat. **Allow to cool** slightly.

Soak the anchovies in a little water to remove the salt, **drain**, and **cut** them neatly in half lengthways.

Preheat the oven to 425°F (220°C/Gas mark 7). **Remove** the stalk from the summer savory and roughly **chop** the leaves. **Spread** the stewed onions over the dough, **arrange** the olives and anchovies on top, and **sprinkle** over the summer savory.

Bake for approximately 10 minutes. **Drizzle** with the remaining olive oil before serving.

BRAISED **CHICKEN** WITH **OLIVES**

POULET AUX OLIVES

Ingredients

1 free-range chicken
1 cup (3 ½ oz./100 g) flour
1 onion
1 bunch young carrots
1 bunch small, young turnips
4 ¼ oz. (120 g) black olives, pitted
4 ¼ oz. (120 g) cracked green olives from Les Baux-de-Provence
3 tablespoons Passedat olive oil*
1 bay leaf
1 tablespoon (15 ml) dry white wine
4 cups (1 liter) chicken stock
Salt, pepper

Serves 4 | *Preparation time: 2 hours* | *Cooking time: 1 hour*

Joint the chicken into eight pieces. **Roll** each piece in the flour, shaking off the excess. **Peel** and **chop** the onion. **Peel** the carrots and turnips and **cut** them in two lengthways.

Soak all the olives in cold water for 5 minutes to remove the salt and then **drain** thoroughly.

Heat the olive oil in a large pan and **brown** the chicken pieces on all sides. **Add** the onion, carrots, turnips, olives, and bay leaf. **Deglaze** with the white wine and **add** the stock. **Season** with salt and pepper and **simmer**, covered, over a medium heat for 1 hour.

Check the seasoning before serving.

GRANDMOTHER MÉLANIE'S GRILLED SCORPION FISH

RASCASSES GRILLÉES DE MAMIE MÉLANIE

Ingredients

2 scorpion fish (or other non-oily, firm-fleshed, gelatinous fish), weighing approximately 14 oz. (400 g) each
1 small bunch summer savory
Scant ½ cup (100 ml) Passedat olive oil*
1 oz. (30 g) *fleur de sel de Camargue* (Camargue sea salt)
12 baby artichokes
3 ½ oz. (100 g) sliced Corsican coppa, or bacon
Salt, pepper

Serves 4 | *Preparation time: 45 minutes* | *Cooking time: 15 minutes*

Clean the fish and **remove** the heads. **Cut** slashes down the side of each one and **insert** sprigs of summer savory into the cuts. **Brush** with olive oil and **season** with the *fleur de sel* and pepper. **Reserve** in the refrigerator.

Wash the artichokes. **Cut off** the stalks and the tips of the leaves. **Make** eight incisions in each with a sharp knife and **insert** strips of the coppa in them. **Brush** with olive oil and **season** with salt and pepper.

Place the fish and the artichokes on a rack over hot coals on a barbecue, **cover**, and **cook** for 15 minutes.

Drizzle the fish and artichokes with olive oil before serving.

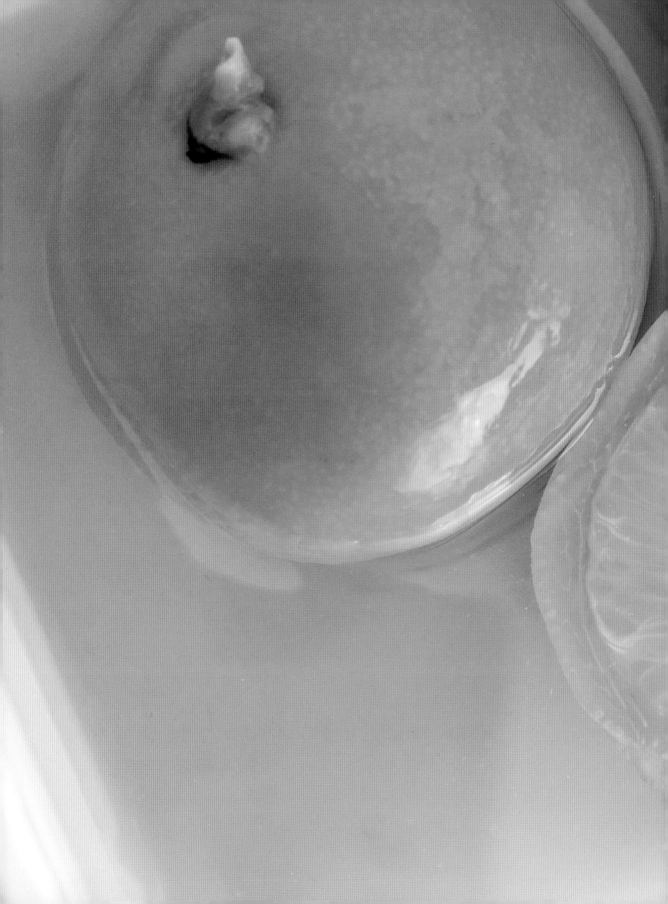

DESSERTS

APRICOTS POACHED IN VANILLA SYRUP WITH ALMOND MILK

ABRICOTS POCHÉS, LAIT D'AMANDE

Ingredients
20 apricots
1 ⅓ cups (9 oz./250 g) sugar
2 cups (500 ml) water
1 vanilla bean
Scant ½ cup (100 ml) milk
1 tablespoon (½ oz./ 15 g) sugar for the almond milk

Serves 4 | *Preparation time: 30 minutes* | *Cooking time: 30 minutes*

Wash the apricots, **cut** them in half, and **remove** the pits. **Reserve** the apricot halves and pits separately.

Make a syrup by putting the 1 ⅓ cups (9 oz./250 g) of sugar and the water in a large pan and heating over a low heat until the sugar dissolves. **Bring to a boil** and **add** the vanilla bean.

Lower the heat under the pan, **add** the apricot halves to the syrup, and **poach** them gently for approximately 15 minutes or until they are very tender but still hold their shape. **Leave** the apricots to cool in the syrup and then **reserve** them in the refrigerator.

Crack the apricot pits and remove the kernels, taking care not to crush them. **Heat** the milk with the remaining 1 tablespoon (½ oz./15 g) sugar, **add** the apricot kernels, and **bring to a boil**. **Pour** the mixture into a liquidizer and **blend** until smooth. **Strain** through a fine-mesh sieve.

Serve the chilled apricots in a deep dish with a little of their syrup spooned over, accompanied by the almond milk.

RED OR GREEN TOMATO JAM

CONFITURES DE TOMATES ROUGES OU VERTES

Ingredients

1 lb. 2 oz. (500 g) red
   or green tomatoes
2 oranges
2 vanilla beans
   (preferably from
   Tahiti)
1 ½ cups (10 oz./300 g)
   sugar

Preparation time: 20 minutes | Cooking time: 1–2 hours

Wash the tomatoes and **remove** their stalks. **Cut** them into chunks and **put** them in a heavy bottomed pan.

Grate the zest from the oranges and **squeeze** the juice. **Split** the vanilla beans lengthways with a sharp knife. **Add** the orange zest and juice and the vanilla beans to the pan with the sugar.

Heat gently until the sugar dissolves, then slowly **bring to a boil** and **cook** over a medium heat for 1–2 hours. **Chill** a saucer in the freezer while the mixture is cooking.

After 1 hour, **test** the jam to see if it has reached setting point. **Take** the pan off the heat to do this. **Put** a teaspoonful of the jam on the chilled saucer, **cool** it for a moment, then **rub** a little of the jam between your finger and thumb and if it sticks to them, it is cooked. If not, **return** the pan to the heat, **cook** the jam for an additional 10 minutes, and then **test** again.

WATERMELON AND CITRUS FRUIT JAM

CONFITURE DE PASTÈQUE ET AGRUMES

Ingredients

2 lb. 4 oz. (1 kg)
   watermelon
2 lemons
2 oranges
2 vanilla beans
   (preferably from
   Tahiti)
Scant 4 cups (1 lb.
   10 oz./750 g) sugar

Preparation time: 20 minutes | Cooking time: 1 hour

Cut the watermelon into quarters, **peel**, and **remove** the seeds. **Reserve** 2 oz. (50 g) of the skin, and **cut** it into squares.

Chop the flesh into pieces and **put** in a large pan. **Grate** the zest and **squeeze** the juice from the citrus fruits. **Split** the vanilla beans lengthways. **Add** the watermelon flesh and chopped skin, citrus juice and zest, and vanilla beans to the pan with the sugar.

Cook over a medium heat for 1 hour, then **check** as for the Tomato Jam recipe above to see if setting point has been reached.

COMPOTE OF CHERRIES IN MUSCAT DE BEAUMES DE VENISE

CERISES AU BEAUMES DE VENISE

Ingredients

7 oz. (200 g) red
   cherries
1 lemon
1 ½ cups (10 oz./300 g)
   sugar
Generous 3 cups
   (800 ml) water
⅓ cup (80 ml) Muscat
   de Beaumes de Venise
   (muscat dessert wine)
2 verbena leaves

Serves 4 | *Preparation time: 10 minutes*

Cut the zest away from the lemon in strips using a potato peeler and **julienne** the strips using a small sharp knife.

Make a syrup with the sugar and the water. **Dissolve** the sugar in the water over a low heat, **bring to a boil**, and **add** the julienne of lemon zest. **Simmer** for a few minutes and then **add** the Beaumes de Venise wine. **Pour** the syrup into a serving bowl and **allow to cool**.

Pit the cherries and **add** them to the cold syrup. **Chop** the verbena finely.

Just before serving, **add** a few ice cubes to the bowl of cherries and **sprinkle** over the chopped verbena.

CALISSONS D'AIX WITH CANDIED LEMON

CALISSONS D'AIX, CITRONS CONFITS

Ingredients

For the almond paste

8 lemons
1 ½ cups (350 ml) water
2 scant cups
   (12 oz./350 g)
   granulated sugar
1 ¾ cups (5 ¼ oz./150 g)
   ground almonds
1 cup (5 oz./140 g)
   confectioners' sugar
1 tablespoon (15 ml)
   Passedat lemon
   vinegar*

For the royal icing

1 tablespoon (15 g)
   egg white
¾ cup (3 ½ oz./100 g)
   confectioners' sugar

Serves 4 | *Preparation time: 2 hours* | *Drying time: 24 hours* | *Cooking time: 3 hours*

Make the almond paste. **Remove** the zest from the lemons in strips using a potato peeler and **squeeze** the juice. **Reserve** 5 oz. (150 g) of zest and **blanch** it by putting it in cold water and bringing it to a boil, then draining and refreshing it under running cold water. **Repeat** this process three times.

When blanched, **put** the zest in a small pan, **cover** with the water, and **add** the granulated sugar. **Heat** gently until the sugar dissolves, then **bring to a simmer** and **leave** over a very low heat for about 3 hours until the strips of zest are crystalized but still soft.

Drain the zest, reserving the syrup. **Reserve** a little of the zest for decoration, cutting it into fine julienne strips. **Put** the remainder in a food processor with a small amount of the reserved syrup and **process** to a paste. **Add** the ground almonds, the confectioners' sugar, and the lemon vinegar and **process** again to bring the ingredients together into a firm but supple paste.

Heat the paste in a pan and **stir** briskly to dry out the mixture. **Remove**, **roll out** evenly between two sheets of parchment paper, and **leave** the mixture to dry for approximately 24 hours in an airy place.

Make the royal icing. **Beat** the egg white and the confectioners' sugar together to make a smooth paste. **Pour** the icing over the rolled-out dough, smoothing it in an even layer with a spatula. **Allow to rest** for 1 hour.

Preheat the oven to 250°F (130°C/Gas mark ½). **Cut** the dough into traditional calisson shapes using a small oval-shaped cutter dipped in water. Carefully **lift** the shapes onto a baking sheet with a spatula and **place** in the oven for 5 minutes to firm up the icing but not color it. **Top** each one with a few spirals of the reserved lemon zest before serving.

BAKED FIGS IN PROVENÇAL ROSÉ WINE

FIGUES ROTIES, ROSÉ DE PROVENCE

Ingredients

8 figs
2 vanilla beans
16 fig leaves
½ stick (2 oz./50 g)
   butter
¼ cup (2 oz./50 g)
   brown sugar
⅔ cup (150 ml)
   Provençal rosé wine
16 wooden cocktail
   sticks or toothpicks

Serves 4 | *Preparation time: 30 minutes* | *Cooking time: 20 minutes*

Cut a cross in the top of each fig. **Cut** both vanilla beans in four and **insert** a piece in each fig. **Wrap** the figs individually in two leaves, fixing the leaves in place with wooden cocktail sticks or toothpicks.

Preheat the oven to 350°F (180°C/Gas mark 4). **Arrange** the figs in a baking dish. **Melt** the butter and **sprinkle** the figs with the brown sugar and the butter. **Pour** over the rosé wine and **cook** the figs for 20 minutes.

Serve hot or cold.

GARIGUETTE STRAWBERRIES WITH FRESH GOAT CHEESE

FRAISES GARIGUETTE ET BROUSSE DU ROVE

Ingredients

1 ¾ cups (14 oz./400 g) brousse du Rove (fresh, soft goat milk curds)

Scant 1 cup (200 ml) whipping cream

½ cup (3 ½ oz./100 g) sugar

24 Gariguette strawberries

Serves 4 | *Preparation time: 10 minutes*

Put the soft cheese, cream, and sugar in a bowl and **whisk** together until smooth. **Put** the mixture in a siphon and **reserve** in the refrigerator.

Wash the strawberries, without removing the hulls. **Slice off** the top quarter from each one and **reserve**. **Make** a hollow in each strawberry using a melon baller.

Siphon a generous amount of the cheese mixture into the hollows and **replace** the reserved strawberry tops.

ANISEED AND ORANGE FLOWER WATER COOKIES

NAVETTES MARSEILLAISES

Ingredients

5 cups (1 lb. 2oz./500 g)
   all-purpose flour
1 ¼ cups (8 oz./230 g)
   sugar
1 pinch salt
5 ¼ oz. (150 g) aniseed
4 eggs, beaten
Scant ¼ cup (50 ml)
   orange flower water
¾ stick (3 oz./75 g)
   butter, softened
Scant ¼ cup (50 ml)
   water
1 teaspoon (5 ml) milk

Serves 4 | *Preparation time: 20 minutes* | *Resting time: 1 hour* | *Cooking time: 5 minutes*

Stir the flour, sugar, salt, and aniseed together in a large bowl. **Add** the eggs, orange flower water, and softened butter. **Mix** together, adding as much of the water as is needed to make a firm dough. **Wrap** in plastic wrap and **let rest** for 1 hour in the refrigerator.

Preheat the oven to 325°F (170°C/Gas mark 3).

Divide the dough into 1 ½ oz. (40 g) pieces. **Roll** each piece into an oval and **pinch** the ends to shape them like small boats (*navettes*).

Make an incision along the length of each one with the point of a knife. **Brush** them with the milk.

Bake for approximately 15 minutes until lightly browned.

ANSE DES ENFERS HERBAL GRANITA

GRANITÉ DE L'ANSE DES ENFERS

Ingredients

For the infusion

Scant ½ cup (100 ml)
Passedat Anse des
Enfers Sans Rose
infusion*

1 cup (250 ml) cold
water

For the sugar syrup

Scant ½ cup (100 ml)
cold water

½ cup (3 ½ oz./100 g)
sugar

Serves 4 | *Preparation time: 20 minutes* | *Infusion time: 24 hours* | *Freezing time: 4 hours*

A day ahead, **make** the infusion to give the flavors time to develop. **Put** the infusion in a bowl with the water and **reserve** in the refrigerator to prevent any bitter flavors developing.

Make the sugar syrup. **Put** the water and sugar in a small saucepan over a medium heat. **Dissolve** the sugar, then **bring to a boil** and **bubble** until the temperature of the syrup reaches 85°F (30°C) on a candy thermometer.

Strain the infusion through a coffee filter paper to remove any deposits and **sweeten** with the sugar syrup, according to personal taste. **Pour** the mixture into a small baking dish and **place** it in the freezer for approximately 4 hours.

Put four small serving dishes in the freezer to chill. Just before serving, **remove** the frozen block of mixture from the freezer and **scrape** a fork over the surface to break the block up into small shavings. **Spoon** into the chilled dishes and **serve** at once.

CHEF'S NOTE

Anse des Enfers is part of my collection of infusions called Life Enhancing Herbals, made with a combination of flowers, roots, leaves, and spices, acting as tonics to aid the digestion.

L'Anse des Enfers is the name of a group of deep-water coves close to Marseille.

ALMOND AND PISTACHIO NOUGAT

NOUGAT BLANC AMANDE ET PISTACHE

Ingredients

1 oz. (30 g) egg white
1 ¼ teaspoons (6 g) superfine sugar
Generous ⅓ cup (4 ½ oz./125 g) honey
¾ cup (5 oz./150 g) granulated sugar
2 ⅓ tablespoons (1 ¼ oz./35 g) liquid glucose
4 tablespoons (60 ml) water
2 ½ tablespoons (1 ¼ oz./35 g) cocoa butter
2 tablespoons (1 oz./30 g) confectioners' sugar
1 cup (6 oz./175 g) whole blanched almonds
⅓ cup (1 ¾ oz./50g) shelled pistachios

Serves 4 | *Preparation time: 1 hour* | *Cooking time: 10 minutes*

Whisk the egg whites with the superfine sugar. **Heat** the honey in a small saucepan until the temperature reaches 250°F (122°C) on a candy thermometer. **Pour** the hot honey over the egg whites in a thin, steady stream, whisking continuously.

Mix the granulated sugar with the liquid glucose and water in the same pan and **heat** to 300°F (150°C). **Pour** this over the meringue, again whisking continuously until stiff and shiny.

Dry out the meringue with the use of a blowtorch for about 5 minutes, depending on the texture of the meringue. **Melt** the cocoa butter and **add** with the confectioners' sugar, before folding in the nuts until evenly incorporated.

Pour the mixture into a stainless steel tray lined with rice paper and **spread** it **out** in an even layer using a spatula. **Chill** until firm before cutting the nougat into shapes of your choice.

VINE PEACHES POACHED IN GREEN TEA SYRUP WITH MINT

PÊCHES DE VIGNE AU THÉ VERT ET À LA MENTHE

Ingredients

2 cups (500 ml) water
⅓ cup (2 oz./60 g) sugar
8 peaches
1 tablespoon green tea
    leaves
10 mint leaves

Serves 4 | *Preparation time: 35 minutes* | *Cooking time: 10 minutes* | *Infusing time: 10 minutes*

Heat the water and sugar in a deep pan until the sugar dissolves. **Bring to a boil**, **add** the whole peaches, and **allow** them **to poach** over a low heat for 10 minutes. **Lift** them **out** with a slotted spoon and **reserve**.

Add the green tea leaves to the syrup while the syrup is still hot, **remove** from the heat, and **allow to infuse** for 10 minutes.

Strain the syrup, discarding the tea leaves. **Pour** the syrup into a large serving bowl and **add** the mint leaves. **Slip** the skins **off** the peaches and **add** them to the syrup. **Chill** in the refrigerator until ready to serve.

PROVENÇAL
LEMON
FRITTERS

OREILLETTES DE PROVENCE

Ingredients

2 lemons from Menton

5 cups (1 lb. 2 oz./
   500 g) all-purpose
   flour

1 teaspoon (5 g) salt

4 eggs

¼ cup (1 ¾ oz./50 g)
   sugar

3 tablespoons (50 ml)
   Passedat olive oil*

Scant tablespoon
   (10 ml) orange
   flower water

4 cups (1 liter)
   grapeseed oil,
   for deep frying

Confectioners' sugar
   for dusting

Serves 4 | *Preparation time: 20 minutes* | *Resting time:*
2 hours | *Cooking time: a few minutes*

Wash the lemons and **grate** their zest into the flour. **Add** all the
other ingredients and **mix** until you have a smooth dough.

Allow to rest for at least 2 hours, covering the bowl with a cloth
to prevent the dough from drying out.

Divide the dough into small balls and **flatten** them as much as
possible with the palm of your hand. Using a serrated wheel cutter,
cut into rectangles measuring ¾ × 4 in. (2 × 10 cm).

Heat the oil in a deep-fat fryer or deep saucepan to 340°F
(170°C) and **deep fry** the fritters until lightly browned. **Remove**
them with a slotted spoon and **drain** on a plate lined with paper
towel.

Sprinkle the fritters with confectioners' sugar and **serve** hot.

CHEF'S NOTE
The finest lemons come from the Mediterranean town of Menton
and I use them to make these traditional fritters.

ÎLE VERTE
SANGRIA

Ingredients

2 oranges

3 cups (750 ml) red
   wine

1 vanilla bean

1 tablespoon (15 g)
   Passedat Île Verte
   infusion*

2 star anise

½ cup (3 ½ oz./100 g)
   sugar

9 oz. (250 g)
   watermelon

1 grapefruit

1 cup (5 oz./150 g) red
   currants

1 bunch white muscat
   grapes

1 bunch black grapes

1 orange-fleshed melon,
   such as canteloupe

Serves 4 | *Preparation time: 15 minutes* | *Cooking time: 10 minutes*

Wash and **quarter** the oranges. **Put** them in a large saucepan
and **add** the red wine, vanilla bean, Île Verte infusion, star anise,
and sugar.

Bring to a boil over a medium heat and **flambé** by removing the
pan from the heat and setting the cooking liquid alight with a taper
or long match. Once the flames have died down, **put** the pan back
over the heat and **allow to bubble** until the liquid has reduced by
half. **Allow to cool.**

Meanwhile, **peel** the watermelon and **remove** any seeds. **Set
aside** some of the flesh, to be added with the other fruits at the end;
put the rest of the flesh in a food processor. **Reduce** to a pulp, **push
through** a sieve, and **reserve.**

Wash and then **remove** the zest from the grapefruit using a
potato peeler. **Blanch** the zest in boiling water, **drain,** and **refresh**
under cold running water. **Divide** the grapefruit into segments.
Wash the red currants and **strip** them from their stalks. **Wash** and
halve the grapes. **Peel** the melon, **deseed** it, and **cut** the flesh into
cubes. **Cut** the reserved watermelon into cubes.

Add the cooled syrup to the watermelon juice, the grapefruit
zest, and all the prepared fruits.

CHEF'S NOTE

*Île Verte is part of my collection of infusions called Life Enhancing
Herbals, made with a combination of flowers, roots, leaves, and spices,
acting as tonics to aid digestion.*

SPICED
HONEY CAKE

PAIN D'ÉPICIER

Ingredients

2 ¼ cups (550 ml) milk

3 sticks (12 oz./350 g)
butter, diced

1 ½ cups (10 oz./300 g)
sugar

1 ⅓ cups (1 lb./450 g)
honey

5 teaspoons (generous
¾ oz./25 g) Passedat
Pain d'Épicier
spice mix*

3 eggs

3 oz. (90 g) candied
orange, finely
chopped

3 ⅛ cups (14 oz./400 g)
all-purpose flour

2 cups (9oz./250 g)
buckwheat flour

Scant 1 tablespoon
(⅜ oz./12 g) baking
soda

¼ teaspoon (1 ¼ g)
fleur de sel

Extra honey for glazing
(optional)

Serves 4 | *Preparation time: 30 minutes* | *Cooking time: 1 hour*

Heat the milk in a saucepan with the butter, sugar, honey, and spice until the butter has melted. **Bring to a boil**, **remove** from the heat, **cover** the pan, and **allow to infuse** for 15 minutes.

Preheat the oven to 340°F (170°C/Gas mark 3) and **line** the base and sides of a 2-lb. (900-g) loaf pan with parchment paper.

Beat the eggs and finely chopped candied orange together in a mixing bowl. **Whisk** in the warm milk mixture, **add** the flours, baking soda, and *fleur de sel*, and **stir** until all the ingredients are evenly combined.

Pour the cake batter into the prepared loaf pan to fill it three-quarters full and **bake** for approximately 1 hour. **Test** by inserting the point of a small knife or a toothpick and if it comes out clean the cake is cooked.

If you wish, you can **glaze** the cake when it comes out of the oven by brushing the top with honey.

CHEF'S NOTE

Pain d'Épicier spice mix is my own blend that I created specially for this cake consisting of cinnamon, ginger, aniseed, cloves, and cardamom.

INDIVIDUAL LICORICE SOUFFLÉS WITH FRESH ALMONDS

SOUFFLÉ À LA RÉGLISSE
ET AMANDES FRAÎCHES

Ingredients

For the pastry cream

6 egg yolks
⅔ cup (4 ½ oz./125 g) sugar
⅓ cup (1 ½ oz./45 g) corn starch
2 cups (500 ml) milk

For the soufflés

2 tablespoons (1 oz./30 g) butter
½ cup (3 ½ oz./100 g) sugar
3 sticks licorice
8 egg whites
12 fresh almonds in their shells

Serves 4 | *Preparation time: 30 minutes* | *Cooking time: 15 minutes*

Make the pastry cream. **Mix** the egg yolks with the sugar and **add** the corn starch, whisking until smooth. **Bring** the milk to a boil in a saucepan and **pour** half of it over the yolks and sugar, whisking vigorously. **Pour** this mixture back into the saucepan and **stir** continuously over a medium heat until thickened and smooth. **Remove** from the heat and **set aside to cool**, stirring occasionally to prevent a skin forming on top.

Make the soufflés. **Melt** the butter and **brush** it over the insides of four individual soufflé dishes. **Sprinkle** with half of the sugar.

Grate the licorice sticks to a powder and **mix** the powder into the pastry cream, reserving a little for sprinkling. **Preheat** the oven to 350°F (180°C/Gas mark 4).

Whisk the egg whites with the remaining sugar and **fold** into the pastry cream with a spatula so they are evenly incorporated and no lumps of egg white remain.

Fill the dishes to the top, **sprinkle** the reserved licorice powder over the soufflés, and **cook** them for 15 minutes in the oven.

Shell the almonds. **Place** three almonds next to each soufflé and **serve** at once.

SWEET OLIVE OIL YEAST CAKE WITH ORANGE FLOWER WATER

POMPE À L'HUILE

Ingredients

4 teaspoons (⅔ oz./ 20 g) baker's yeast

3 cups (10 oz./300 g) all-purpose flour

⅓ cup (75 ml) Passedat olive oil*

⅓ cup (2 ⅔ oz./80 g) sugar

1 egg

⅓ teaspoon (2 g) salt

2 tablespoons (30 ml) orange flower water

Finely grated zest of 1 orange

2 tablespoons (30 ml) water

1 egg yolk

Serves 4 | *Preparation time: 45 minutes* | *Resting time: 6 hours* | *Cooking time: 10–15 minutes*

Make a starter dough. **Dissolve** the yeast in a little warm water with 1 cup (3 ½ oz./100 g) of the flour. **Set aside to rest** for 2 hours at room temperature, free from drafts.

When the starter dough is ready, **prepare** the rest of the dough. **Put** the remaining flour into a food processor fitted with a dough hook and **add** the olive oil, sugar, whole egg, salt, orange flower water, orange zest, and water. **Knead** on the lowest speed for 2 minutes, then **add** the starter dough and **mix** it in well.

Take the dough out of the food processor, **wrap** it in a cloth, and **allow** it **to rise** for 3 hours at room temperature, free from drafts.

When the dough has risen, **punch** it **down** with your fist to remove any air trapped inside it, then **knead** thoroughly with your hands until it is smooth and elastic. **Divide** the dough in half and **flatten** each half into an oval shape. **Place** on a baking sheet, **cut** diagonal slashes in the dough with the point of a knife, **cover** with a cloth, and **let rise** again for 1 hour.

Preheat the oven to 300°F (150°C/Gas mark 2). **Brush** the risen dough with the egg yolk and **cook** for 10–15 minutes with a bowl of water placed on the floor of the oven, so the dough bakes in a moist heat.

FLOURLESS ORANGE AND ALMOND CAKE

TARTE À L'ORANGE

Ingredients

7 oranges

6 eggs

1 cup (7 oz./200 g) sugar

3 cups (9 oz./250 g) ground almonds

1 teaspoon (5 g) baking powder

2 teaspoons (10 ml) orange flower water

Juice of 1 lemon

Butter and flour for the cake pan

Slices of candied orange for decoration (optional)

Serves 4 | *Preparation time: 30 minutes* | *Cooking time: 1 hour 30 minutes*

Place the oranges in a large saucepan and **cover** with water. **Bring to a boil** and **cook** for 1 hour over medium heat, topping up the pan with extra boiling water, if necessary, so the oranges remain immersed.

Drain the oranges, **cut** them into quarters, discarding any seeds, and **reduce** them to a purée in a blender or food processor: you should have 1 lb. 2 oz. (500 g) of orange pulp.

Put the eggs and sugar in the bowl of an electric food mixer fitted with a whisk attachment and **beat** until thick, creamy, and pale in color. **Fold in** the ground almonds and baking powder using a spatula. Gradually **fold in** the 1 lb. 2 oz. (500 g) of orange purée, followed by the orange flower water.

Preheat the oven to 325°F (160°C/Gas mark 3). **Butter** a deep, round 12 in. (30 cm) cake pan with a removable base and **dust** with flour.

Pour the cake batter into the pan and **bake** for 30 minutes. **Allow to settle** for a few minutes, then carefully **remove** the cake from the pan and **spoon** over the lemon juice.

You can **decorate** the cake with thin slices of candied orange as a finishing touch.

MENTON LEMON TART

TARTE AUX CITRONS DE MENTON

Ingredients

For the sweet pastry crust

Generous 1 ¼ sticks
(5 ¼ oz./150 g) butter,
diced
2 ½ cups (9 oz./250 g)
all-purpose flour
1 pinch salt
⅓ cup (1 oz./30 g)
ground almonds
¾ cup (3 ⅓ oz./95 g)
confectioners' sugar
1 egg, beaten

For the lemon cream filling

8 lemons
12 eggs
2 ⅓ cups (15 ½ oz./
440 g) superfine
sugar
4 leaves gelatin
3 sticks (12 oz./340 g)
butter, softened

For the candied lemons

5 lemons
1 ⅓ cups (9 oz./250 g)
sugar
1 ¼ cups (300 ml) water
Zest of 1 lime

Serves 4 | *Preparation time: 40 minutes* | *Resting time: 3 hours* | *Cooking time: 20 minutes*

Make the pastry. In a large mixing bowl, **rub** the butter into the flour until the mixture resembles fine bread crumbs. **Add** in the salt and ground almonds, **sift in** the confectioners' sugar, and **stir** to combine. **Mix in** the egg to make a smooth dough. **Wrap** in plastic wrap and **let rest** for 2 hours in the refrigerator.

Make the lemon cream filling. **Wash** the lemons, **grate** the zest from four, and **reserve**. **Juice** all eight lemons, measure 1 ⅔ cups (400 ml), and **pour** into a saucepan. **Add** the zest, and heat gently.

Beat the eggs and superfine sugar together until light and pale, **pour** the hot lemon juice over them, and **return** to the pan. **Heat** gently, stirring constantly. **Cook** for 1 minute.

Soak the gelatin leaves in a bowl of cold water. When soft, **drain** well and **add** to the lemon cream, stirring until dissolved. **Transfer** to the bowl of a food processor and **allow to cool** to 100°F (40°C). **Add** the butter and **process** until very smooth. **Transfer** to a bowl and **reserve** in the refrigerator **once cool**.

Make the candied lemon slices. **Wash** the lemons and **slice** them on a mandolin. **Remove** the seeds. **Make** a syrup with the sugar and water by heating them gently in a saucepan until the sugar has dissolved. **Immerse** the lemon slices in the syrup and **allow** them **to candy** over a low heat until the peel is translucent. **Cool**, then **lift** the lemon slices out of the syrup and reserve.

Butter a 12 in. (30 cm) tart mold , **roll out** the pastry thinly, and **line** the mold with it. **Let rest** in the refrigerator for at least 1 hour.

Preheat the oven to 340°F (170°C/Gas mark 3) and **bake** the tart shell blind for 12 minutes. **Remove** from the oven and **allow to cool**.

Spoon the lemon cream filling into a pastry bag fitted with a plain tip and **pipe** it into the tart shell, smoothing the top level with a spatula. **Decorate** with candied lemon slices and lime zest.

SOFT SET LAVENDER YOGURT WITH ARLETTE COOKIES

TREMBLANT LAVANDE ET ARLETTES

Ingredients

For the lavender yogurt

4 cups (2 lb. 2 oz./ 960 g) plain yogurt

½ cup (3 ½ oz./100 g) sugar

5 sprays fresh lavender

⅖ teaspoon (1.8 g) agar-agar

For the arlette cookies

7 oz. (200 g) puff pastry dough, ready prepared

Sugar and ground cinnamon for sprinkling

Generous cup (5 ¼ oz./150 g) confectioners' sugar

Serves 4 | Preparation time: 45 minutes | Infusion time: 30 minutes | Resting time: 4 hours 30 minutes | Cooking time: 10 minutes

Make the lavender yogurt. **Put** the yogurt in a pan and **bring to a boil** with the sugar, then **strain** through butter muslin over a bowl. **Wash** the lavender and **infuse** in the strained liquid (whey) for 30 minutes. **Strain** through a fine-mesh sieve into a small saucepan and **add** the agar-agar. **Bring to a boil, skim,** then **pour** into four individual ramekins.

Allow to set at room temperature for 1 hour, then **place** in the refrigerator for at least 3 hours.

Make the arlette cookies. **Flatten** the block of puff pastry dough with a rolling pin, **brush** it with water, and then **sprinkle** with the sugar and ground cinnamon.

Roll out the dough thinly on a sheet of parchment paper and **let** it **rest** in the refrigerator for 15 minutes.

Cut the dough into ½ in. (1 cm) pieces. **Sprinkle** the confectioners' sugar on a cool surface and **roll out** each piece individually into a thin oval shape.

Place the ovals on a baking sheet lined with parchment paper. **Cover** with a second sheet of parchment paper and **place** a second baking sheet on top to prevent the pastry rising in the oven. **Allow to rest** for 10 minutes in the refrigerator.

Preheat the oven to 340°F (170°C/Gas mark 3). **Bake** the cookies for approximately 10 minutes, depending on their size and thickness.

Serve the lavender yogurts accompanied by the arlette cookies.

MELON SLICES WITH VERBENA AND SECHUAN PEPPER

TRANCHE DE MELON, VERBENA ET POIVRE TIMUT

Ingredients

⅔ cup (150 ml) water
¾ cup (5 ¼ oz./150 g)
  sugar
1 small bunch fresh
  verbena
4 teaspoons (20 g)
  Sechuan peppercorns
2 Cavaillon melons,
  or other orange-flesh
  melons, such
  as canteloupe

Serves 4 | *Preparation time: 10 minutes* | *Infusion time: 20 minutes* | *Cooking time: 5 minutes*

Heat the water and sugar in a small saucepan until the sugar dissolves. **Bring to a boil**, **remove** from the heat, and **add** the verbena and the peppercorns. **Cover** the pan and **allow to infuse** for 20 minutes.

Strain the infusion and **reserve**. **Discard** the peppercorns, reserving the verbena leaves for garnishing.

Peel the melons and discard the seeds. **Cut** the flesh into thin slices and shape them into rectangles. **Place** the rectangles side by side and upright in a serving dish. **Cut** each verbena leaf in two, and **insert** a half leaf between each rectangle of melon.

Serve with the infusion poured around the melon.

ICED ALLUMETTES WITH STRAWBERRIES AND GREEK YOGURT

ALLUMETTES ROYALES, FRAISES DES BOIS ET YAOURT GREC

Ingredients

2 cups (1 lb./480 g)
   Greek yogurt
1 lime
1 lemon
6 ½ tablespoons
   (1 ⅔ oz./50 g)
   Passedat Divin
   Aigrelet spice mix*
1 ⅓ cups (7 oz./200 g)
   wild strawberries
7 oz. (200 g) puff
   pastry dough,
   ready prepared

For the royal icing

1 tablespoon (15 g)
   egg white
¾ cup (3 ½ oz./100 g)
   confectioners' sugar

Serves 4 | *Preparation time: 20 minutes* | *Freezing time: 10 minutes* | *Cooking time: 8 minutes*

Put the yogurt in a large bowl.

Grate the zest from the lemon and lime into the bowl. **Juice** the lime and **add** to the bowl with the Divin Aigrelet spice. Carefully **mix** everything into the yogurt and then **pour** into four ramekins.

Wash the wild strawberries.

Make the royal icing. **Whisk** the egg white and confectioners' sugar together until smooth and glossy.

Roll out the puff pastry. **Spread** the royal icing over the pastry using a spatula. **Let** it **rest** in the refrigerator for 10 minutes.

Preheat the oven to 340°F (170°C/Gas mark 3).

Cut the puff pastry into matchsticks approximately 5 × ½ in. (12 × 1 cm).

Bake the allumettes for approximately 8 minutes, depending on their thickness.

Serve the spiced yogurt accompanied by the wild strawberries and the iced allumettes.

CHEF'S NOTE

Divin Aigrelet spice mix is a blend from my range of spices, consisting of brown sugar, lavender flowers, and powdered vanilla.

FIG
TART

TARTE AUX FIGUES

Ingredients

14 oz. (400 g) black figs

For the sweet shortcrust pastry

¾ stick (3 oz./85 g) butter, diced and softened

5 tablespoons (2 ½ oz./70 g) superfine sugar

1 pinch (1 g) *fleur de sel*

Scant 1 cup (3 ½ oz./100 g) flour

1 teaspoon (5 g) Passedat Mélange Agaçant spice mix*

1 egg yolk

For the almond cream

⅔ cup (2 ⅓ oz./65 g) ground almonds

⅓ cup (2 ⅓ oz./65 g) light brown sugar

4 ½ tablespoons (2 ⅓ oz./65 g) butter, diced and softened

1 egg

To decorate

3 tablespoons (50 g) honey

1 dried fig

A few flaked almonds

Zest of 1 orange

Serves 4 | *Preparation time: 30 minutes* | *Resting time: 30 minutes* | *Cooking time: 25 minutes*

Make the pastry. **Put** the butter in a bowl with the sugar and *fleur de sel*. **Beat** them together with a wooden spoon or spatula until smooth and creamy. Gradually **work in** the flour and spice mixture and then the egg yolk to make a soft dough. **Reserve**.

Make the almond cream. **Put** the ground almonds in a bowl with the sugar and softened butter and **beat** them for 5 minutes. **Add** the egg and continue to **mix** thoroughly until the mixture is smooth and all the ingredients are evenly combined. **Reserve**.

Flatten the pastry into a round, **place** it in a 12 in. (30 cm) tart mold , and **press** it **out** thinly with your fingertips until it covers the base and sides of the mold in an even layer of $^1/_8$ in. (3 mm). **Let rest** in the refrigerator for 30 minutes.

Preheat the oven to 350°F (180°C/Gas mark 4). **Bake** the tart shell blind for approximately 10 minutes until it is cooked through but not colored. **Allow to cool**.

Meanwhile, **wash** the figs and **cut** them vertically into thin slices.

Spread a thin layer of almond cream into the tart shell and **arrange** the figs on top, tightly overlapping the slices. **Return** to the oven and **bake** for approximately 15 minutes.

Melt the honey in a small saucepan over a very low heat. **Slice** the dried fig thinly.

Remove the cooked tart from its mold and **brush** the surface with the honey. **Arrange** the dried fig slices and almonds on top. **Sprinkle** over the orange zest and **serve** while still warm.

CHEF'S NOTE

In Provence, the verb "agacer" means "to titillate" and it is said in a way that no one can mistake its meaning! Here, the taste of the fruit is enhanced—or titillated—by the addition of my Mélange Agaçant spice mix, made up of cinnamon, ginger, nutmeg, cloves, and a hint of vanilla.

INDEX

OF RECIPES

INDEX

OF PRODUCTS

ACKNOWLEDGMENTS

This book of recipes, designed for home cooking and for sharing, is dedicated to my family and their appreciation of fine food, to the traditions of Marseille and Provence, and, of course, to my Mediterranean heritage.

I wish to thank everyone who works alongside me at my restaurants, Le Môle Passedat and Le Petit Nice Passedat, in particular chefs Denis Maillet, Philippe Moreno, Sébastien Tantot, Sébastien Dugast, Christophe Droulin (known to us all as Quito), and Christopher Bignon.

I would also like to thank Catherine Bienvenu, Marie Lamy, Marilou Preschey, and Nelly Bataille.

A special mention must go to Richard Haughton for his keen photographer's eye.

I also extend my thanks to Myriam Boisaubert and Rudy Ricciotti for the warmest of welcomes in their haven of peace.

And, closer to home, thank you to Julie and my son Romeo for their support, and to my loyal dog, Favouille, for his unconditional love.